COMPLETE LESSON PLANS

W9-BEI-195

HEATH

DISCOVERING FRENCH

BLEU

McDougal Littell

A HOUGHTON MIFFLIN COMPANY

Evanston, Illinois • Boston • Dallas

Copyright © 1998 by D.C. Heath and Company, a Division of Houghton Mifflin Company.

All rights reserved. Permission to reproduce these pages is granted to users of *Discovering French*.

Printed in the United States of America.

International Standard Book Number: 0-395-87998-1

5 6 7 8 9 0 -DAA- 02 01

CONTENTS

Introduction   v

Cultural Photo Essay Parlons français!   1

Unité 1   Bonjour!
  Leçon 1   La rentrée   3
  Leçon 2   Tu es français?   5
  Leçon 3   Salut! Ça va?   7
  Leçon 4   Le français pratique: L'heure   9

Unité 2   Les copains et la famille
  Leçon 5   Copain ou copine?   11
  Leçon 6   Une coïncidence   13
  Leçon 7   Les photos d'Isabelle   15
  Leçon 8   Le français pratique: Le jour et la date   17

Unité 3   Bon appétit!
  Leçon 9   Tu as faim?   19
  Leçon 10   Au café   21
  Leçon 11   Ça fait combien?   23
  Leçon 12   Le français pratique: Le temps   25

Cultural Photo Essay À l'école en France   27

Unité 4   Qu'est-ce qu'on fait?
  Leçon 13   Le français pratique: Mes activités   29
  Leçon 14   Qui est là?   31
  Leçon 15   Une boum   33
  Leçon 16   Une interview   35

Unité 5   Le monde personnel et familier
  Leçon 17   Le français pratique: Les personnes
                 et les objets   37
  Leçon 18   Vive la différence!   39
  Leçon 19   Le copain de Mireille   41
  Leçon 20   La voiture de Roger   43

Unité 6   En ville

Leçon 21	Le français pratique: La ville et la maison	45
Leçon 22	Weekend à Paris	47
Leçon 23	Au Café de l'Univers	49
Leçon 24	Mes voisins	51

Cultural Photo Essay   À Paris   53

Unité 7   Le shopping

Leçon 25	Le français pratique: L'achat des vêtements	55
Leçon 26	Rien n'est parfait!	57
Leçon 27	Un choix difficile	59
Leçon 28	Alice a un job	61

Unité 8   Le temps libre

Leçon 29	Le français pratique: Le weekend et les vacances	63
Leçon 30	Vive le weekend!	65
Leçon 31	L'alibi	67
Leçon 32	Qui a de la chance?	69

Unité 9   Les repas

Leçon 33	Le français pratique: Les repas et la nourriture	71
Leçon 34	À la cantine	73
Leçon 35	Un client difficile	75
Leçon 36	Pique-nique	77

Additional Sample Lesson Plans, including block scheduling options, are located following page 78.

These lesson plans were designed to help both beginning and experienced teachers by providing an overall framework for translating a **Discovering French–Bleu** lesson to a teacher's daily plans.

Description of the lesson plans

Each lesson plan follows the same format:

❑ *Objectives* serve to remind the teacher of the communicative, linguistic, and cultural goals of each lesson.

❑ *Motivation and Focus* provides an introduction to the lesson, activating students' background knowledge about topics to be presented, and discussing cultural situations to make comparisons and to link language and culture.

❑ *Presentation and Explanation* introduces the new material of the lesson. Vocabulary, expressions, and grammatical structures are presented in a cultural context, usually a conversation. Then the separate components are explained, giving students a chance to think critically about the language.

❑ *Guided Practice and Checking Understanding* provides focused practice, from listening comprehension to oral exchanges and readings.

❑ *Independent Practice* allows students to apply vocabulary, expressions, and grammar to communicate their own ideas in role plays, interviews, information gap activities, and reading and writing practice.

❑ *Monitoring and Adjusting* suggests ways teachers can ensure that students understand the language and learn what has been taught.

❑ *Assessment* gives suggestions for formal assessment at the end of each lesson and unit.

❑ *Reteaching* provides suggestions for helping students who have not mastered the material.

❑ *Extension and Enrichment* provides culture-based activities that give additional practice in reading and writing, as well as extra assignments and projects.

❑ *Summary and Closure* allows students to recall and further assimilate what they have learned in the lesson.

❑ *End-of-Lesson/End-of-Unit Activities: À votre tour!* activities give students a chance to review and apply the vocabulary and structures to act out situations, create conversations, and develop role plays. *Entracte,* at the end of each unit, gives students a chance to read for pleasure and to interpret real-life reading materials. The *Entracte* activities also allow students to use critical thinking skills and to make cultural observations. Writing activities give students a chance to express their thoughts and to personalize their language learning experience.

It is advantageous to use a variety of materials in addition to the **Student Textbook**. The **Discovering French** program facilitates this in several ways:

❑ The integrated **Audio/Video (Audiocassette, Audio CD, Video**, and **Videodisc)** components make it easy to incorporate technology into the program in ways that support and extend the work done with the textbook. Both the **Audio** and **Video** can be used to preview lessons, both as a motivational activity and to encourage students' expectations about the lesson. Many of the **Student Textbook** exercises are on both the **Audio** and **Video**, making these forms of technology useful for modeling exercises, checking students' answers, and reviewing material. The **Video**, in particular, is an excellent format for presenting cultural situations and having students comment on similarities and differences between French and American culture. Complete transcriptions of the **Audio** and **Video** sound tracks are available in the **Cassette Script** and **Video Script** books.

❑ The **Extended Teacher's Edition** provides an abundance of suggestions for extension activities, extra projects, cross-curricular connections, and real-world applications. In addition, there are resources and suggestions for using practice activities, Total Physical Response, cooperative learning, critical thinking, and portfolio assessment.

❑ The **Activity Book** and **Video Activity Book** provide guided practice exercises, both oral and written, to complement each lesson's goals. Used with the **Audio** or **Video** (or **Cassette Script** and **Video Script**), these activity books lead students from listening comprehension exercises to communicative and critical thinking activities. Written exercises can be used for independent practice. There is a **Teacher's Annotated Edition** of the **Activity Book**; answers to the **Video Activity Book** activities are included in the back of the book.

❏ Additional role plays, information gap exercises, interviews, conversations, and pairwork activities in **Communipak** provide opportunities for independent communicative practice. Students work in small groups or in pairs on specific assignments.

❏ The **Teacher's Resource Package** provides materials for reteaching, independent practice, and extension and enrichment. Students can monitor and assess their own progress by using the **Answer Key** to check their work. It contains answers for both the **Activity Book** and **Communipak. Teaching to Multiple Intelligences** and **Teacher to Teacher** give suggestions, puzzles, and worksheets that reinforce and reteach language, helping teachers reach all students by addressing various learning styles and needs in the classroom. **Internet Connection Notes** allows students to explore and experience the French-speaking world through the Internet. **Interdisciplinary/Community Connections** provides projects and research activities that make students aware of how French is connected to other subject areas, to their local community, and to the world community.

❏ **Overhead Visuals: Copymasters and Activities** contains complete blackline versions of all overhead visuals. These transparencies can be used to present and practice new vocabulary and structures, and for reteaching and summarizing material. There are also supplementary situational overhead visuals that can be used to integrate functions, vocabulary, and themes. The activity section of the book includes a description of each visual, suggestions for review and practice activities, and expansion activities correlated to the national Goals and Standards for Foreign Language Learning.

❏ The **Testing and Assessment Kit** contains **Achievement Tests, Proficiency Tests**, and forms for **Portfolio Assessment**. Achievement tests include **Lesson Quizzes, Unit Tests**, and **Comprehensive (Semester) Tests**; any of them can be modified, or new tests can be created, using the **Test Bank**. Proficiency tests for **Listening Comprehension, Speaking, Reading**, and **Writing** can be administered at the end of each unit to see how well students can use French to communicate. Portfolio assessment is facilitated by the use of forms for contents, student instructions, and evaluation sheets for both Oral and Written Portfolios.

❏ The **CD-ROM** includes one module for each lesson, containing video and interactive activities that can be used for presentation of material, individual practice and review, small-group work, and testing. Students can record oral and written responses for self-assessment. In addition, the **CD-ROM** may be used to present material to students who have missed class.

❏ **Writing Templates** give students a chance to express their thoughts and to develop writing skills with pre- and postwriting activities and process writing development.

Using the lesson plans

These lesson plans follow the general sequence of a **Discovering French** lesson. However, since they are not daily plans, they are not totally sequential. For example, *Monitoring and Adjusting* and *Reteaching* activities should be used at any appropriate time during the lesson. Teachers should be flexible with the plans, adjusting them to fit their personal teaching styles, the class's specific needs, and the type of scheduling with which they are working.

Teachers using these plans should become familiar with both the overall structure of a **Discovering French–Bleu** lesson and with the format of the lesson plans and available ancillaries before translating these plans to a daily sequence.

Traditional scheduling

For teachers working with 45- or 50-minute class periods, a lesson can be completed in approximately 4–5 days. The different format of different lessons in a unit means that not all lessons will be completed in the same number of days. At this pace, most of the activities in each lesson can be done, but it may not be possible to cover all the lessons included in the book. However, finishing the book is not essential. It is more important to establish an environment in which students know they can use their new language for authentic communication, in which they are willing to take risks while using the language, and in which there is time for activities and projects that make the language come alive. The 5-day lesson model should be considered a model only, to be changed as needed according to each teacher's experience, students, and classroom conditions.

The general format of the 5-day lesson model is as follows:

Day 1:   Do *Motivation and Focus*. Begin *Presentation and Explanation*.

Day 2:   Finish *Presentation and Explanation*. Begin *Guided Practice and Checking Understanding*.

Day 3:   Finish *Guided Practice and Checking Understanding*. Do *Independent Practice*.

Day 4:   Do *Monitoring and Adjusting*. Do *Assessment*.

Day 5:   Do *Reteaching*. Do *Extension and Enrichment*. Do *Summary and Closure*.

The lessons in *Niveau A* (Units 1–3) are much shorter than those in Units 4–9. *Niveau A* lessons can be completed in approximately 2 days. Again, pacing may vary according to the classroom situation.

Block scheduling

Block scheduling can mean different things in different places. In some versions of block scheduling, classes meet every other day for two semesters ("AB" scheduling). In other versions, classes meet every day for one semester ("4 x 4" scheduling). What all types of block scheduling have in common is that class periods are longer; they are double, or almost double, the length of a traditional period.

Longer periods can provide numerous advantages to foreign language teachers. They allow the kind of intense exposure to the language that helps make immersion teaching so successful. With less time spent on beginning- and end-of-class housekeeping tasks, block scheduling gives students more time on task and facilitates more in-depth coverage of content. Longer periods also give teachers more time to focus students' attention on the language and to provide the practice needed to be able to use the language. Teachers find they have plenty of time for pair and group work without sacrificing explanation and teacher-directed practice. Finally, longer periods allow for extra projects and activities that motivate students to use their new language. Whether it's writing and producing videos, exchanging cultural packages with a French-speaking class somewhere, or producing a French talent show, block scheduling gives teachers the flexibility needed to do the kinds of long-term, hands-on projects that make the language real for students.

Although block scheduling can help foreign language teachers be more successful, teachers working with block scheduling face a challenge. Experienced teachers may find that doing the same activities for longer periods of time does not always work. Beginning teachers may have a hard time keeping students' attention for 90 minutes at a time. For all teachers, the key to successful implementation of block scheduling is careful planning. Without careful planning, the extra time provided by longer periods is wasted, and the advantages of block scheduling are lost.

In planning for block scheduling, it is helpful to think about the traditional separation of foreign language teaching activities into "skill getting" and "skill using." Skill-getting activities, while necessary, have no authentic purpose beyond practice. They should be short and as varied as possible in order to maintain students' interest. Skill-using activities are things for which students might use the language in the real world; they have an authentic purpose. These activities should take advantage of the longer periods of time that block scheduling allows. Planning for block scheduling should include both shorter, more varied activities (skill-getting), and longer, more intensive activities (skill-using).

In planning both skill-getting and skill-using activities, teachers working with block scheduling will find it advantageous to use the variety of ancillary materials available with the ***Discovering French*** program. One very effective way to do this is to set up a variety of work stations around the room, where students can work independently, in pairs, and in small groups on activities using the **Audio**, **Video**, **CD-ROM**, **Activity Books**, **Communipak**, and **Answer Key**.

Model daily lesson plan

Following is a model daily lesson plan for a traditional 50-minute class period. For different ways of preparing a lesson, including block scheduling, refer to the *Sample Lesson Plans* found at the end of this book.

Unit 4, Lesson 13
Day 1:

❏ *Part Opener* and *Unit Opener* (pages 84–87): Discuss the photos and read the *Thème et objectifs*. Discuss similarities and differences between French and American activities. Do the CROSS-CULTURAL OBSERVATION and share PHOTO CULTURE NOTE information on page T87.

❏ **Interdisciplinary/Community Connections:** Assign Project Four (pages 54–57). Have students begin planning their projects.

❏ *Lesson Opener:* Read *Accent sur...* (page 88). Discuss typical activities of French teenagers mentioned in the selection and shown in the photos. Help students read the photo captions. Ask students about their favorite activities. Do PHOTO CULTURE NOTES on page T89.

❏ *Vocabulary A:* Play **Video** 13.1–2 or **Audio** 13.1 or model the expressions in *Préférences*, pages 90–91. Use **Overhead Visuals** Transparencies 14a and b. Help students talk about their own likes and dislikes using the expressions.

❏ *Vocabulary B:* Present *Souhaits*, page 93. Model the expressions in this section and have students repeat. Guide students to talk about their own wishes.

❏ *Vocabulary C:* Model *Invitations*, page 94. Play **Video** 13.3 or **Audio** 13.3–4 and have students repeat the questions and expressions. Use gestures to clarify meanings of expressions for accepting and turning down an invitation.

Homework: Have students study *Vocabulary A, B,* and *C* (pages 90–94), and re-read *Accent sur...* (page 88).

Day 2:

❏ Check homework by giving a short vocabulary quiz.

❏ Compare French and American public telephone systems. Play **Video** 13.5 or read **Video Script**, page 26, to present information on the French telephone system.

❏ **Overhead Visuals:** Use Transparencies S9 and 14a and b, and activities on pages A18 and A64–A65. Have students practice talking about preferences, wishes, and invitations.

❏ **Activity Book** (pages 89–92): Use **Audio** or the **Cassette Script** to do activities B–F for listening comprehension.

Homework: Have students prepare textbook activities 1, 3, 4, 8, and 9 on pages 90–94 for oral presentation; they should write activities 2, 5, 6, and 7.

Day 3:

❏ TPR: Do the activity on page T90 to practice talking about everyday activities.

❏ **Video Activity Book:** Play the **Video** or read from the **Video Script** as students do activities 1–6 on pages 49–52.

❏ Check written homework. Do the ORAL INTRODUCTION activity on page T90 before doing activity 1 as COOPERATIVE GROUP PRACTICE as explained on page T91. Have students do practice activities 3, 4, 8, and 9, pages 92–94, in pairs. Students can check their answers in the **Answer Key**.

❏ **Communipak:** Have students work in pairs on Échange 1, page 61, and/or Tête à tête 1, pages 63–64.

Homework: Activity Book: Assign the Writing Activities on pages 105–106.

Day 4:

❏ Check homework.

❏ Based on students' performance on practice activities and homework, refer students back to the vocabulary boxes on pages 90–91, 93, and 94. Use suggestions from pages T90–T94 as needed.

❏ **Teaching to Multiple Intelligences** (pages 57–58): Do activity 1 to review verbs.

❏ Do Quiz 13 on pages 55–56 of **Lesson Quizzes**.

Homework: Have students redo any textbook or **Activity Book** activities as needed, or do activities from the **Writing Template** or **CD-ROM**.

Day 5:

❏ Check homework. Go over the **Lesson Quiz**.

❏ Reteach as needed, using the **Activity Book**, **CD-ROM**, and/or **Video**.

❏ **Internet Connection Notes:** Do project 1 or 2 on pages 27–30 to explore sites for recreational activities.

❏ **Overhead Visuals** Transparency S9: Ask students to present role plays for the Goal 1 activity on page A18. Summarize the communicative functions of the lesson.

❏ *À votre tour!*: Arrange students in pairs for activities 1–3, page 95.

Homework: Assign *À votre tour!* activities 4–5, page 95. Activity 5 can be included in students' Written Portfolios (see pages 2–3 of **Portfolio Assessment**).

CULTURAL PHOTO ESSAY: *Parlons français!*, PAGE XIV

Objectives

Cultural Goals To appreciate the multi-cultural and multi-racial diversity of the French-speaking world

To gain awareness of the importance of French as a global language

To gain knowledge of France's geographic diversity, long history, technological sophistication, and important contributions to the arts, philosophy, and literature

Note: This Cultural Photo Essay provides activities to help students consider why French is important and to motivate students to learn the language. You may want to refer back to it throughout this level as various French-speaking countries are mentioned.

Motivation and Focus

❏ Begin by asking students to look through the pictures on pages i–xii and 1–9. Discuss why they chose to study French, and what they know about products, people, and places associated with France. Remind them of French connections they may have studied about in social studies and in the arts, such as explorers, inventors and scientists, and artists. Guide students to talk about contemporary French influences in cars, fashion, food, and technology.

❏ Have students suggest countries where French is spoken. Then show **Overhead Visuals** Transparency 2a, and compare their responses with those indicated on the world map.

❏ As an overview of *Parlons français!*, play **Video** sections A.1–A.4. Pause occasionally to allow students to comment on people and places.

Presentation and Explanation

❏ To present the detailed extent of the French-speaking world, use **Overhead Visuals** Transparencies 2b and c. Call attention to French influence on all the major continents. Read together pages 4–5, helping students pronounce the names of the French-speaking countries. Discuss the CULTURAL NOTE and CULTURAL EXPANSION information in the TE margins.

❏ Have students look at pages 2–3 in the textbook. Do the PRE-READING activity on page T2 encouraging students to guess where the people are from in the French-speaking world. Ask students to read the interviews; assist with names.

❏ Ask students to look at the map of France, page 6. Students can point out major rivers, mountain ranges, and cities. Have students identify surrounding countries and bodies of water. Ask students to read the facts on page 7. Encourage them to consider how and why France has been important throughout history. Share additional information from the PHOTO CULTURE NOTES and CULTURAL NOTES on pages T6–T7.

❏ As students look through the lists of French names on pages 8–9, have them comment on names that they recognize or that are similar to English names. Use the TEACHING NOTE on the bottom of page T9 to help with pronunciation of the names.

Guided Practice and Checking Understanding

❏ Have students locate the countries mentioned in the interviews on pages 2–3 on a world map: use either **Overhead Visuals** Transparencies 2a–c or pages R2–R3 in the textbook. Do the POST-READING ACTIVITY at the bottom of page T2.

❏ Say the different regions of France and ask students to point to the regions of France on **Overhead Visuals** Transparency 1 without looking in their books.

❏ Follow the suggestions on page 48 of the Teacher's Edition to introduce INITIAL TPR (Total Physical Response) ACTIVITIES. Practice classroom objects and commands with TPR ACTIVITY 1 and 2.

Independent Practice

❑ Have students choose any or all of the *Activités culturelles* on pages 3, 5, and 7 to prepare for homework. Students can share their responses with the class.

❑ Assign **Teacher to Teacher**, page 1, unscrambling French-speaking country names.

Monitoring and Adjusting

❑ As students name French-speaking countries on the world map on pages R2–R3, monitor pronunciation. Say the names and have students repeat as needed.

❑ To find out about students' interests and learning styles, use **Teaching to Multiple Intelligences** activity 1 on pages 7–9. The information can be used to adapt future lesson content and your teaching methods to your class's learning styles.

Assessment

❑ Informally assess students' listening skills as you do the INITIAL TPR ACTIVITIES on page 48 of the Teacher's Edition.

❑ To check familiarity with French-speaking countries, show **Overhead Visuals** Transparencies 2a and b and ask students to locate the native countries of the people mentioned on pages 2–3.

Reteaching

❑ Use Transparencies 1 and 2a to reteach French geographical features and French-speaking countries. Play the game on page A42 in **Overhead Visuals**.

❑ Using the photos on pages 2–3, say "*Je m'appelle ___.*" Ask students to identify the number of the photo that corresponds to the name you said, and to find the country the person is from on the map on pages 4–5.

Extension and Enrichment

❑ To help develop an awareness of French-speaking countries of the world, have students work on a research project: a bulletin board display of France as described in CLASSROOM PROJECT at the bottom of page T6, or a brief research of one of the items listed in the CULTURAL NOTES on page T7.

Summary and Closure

❑ Revisit the maps in **Overhead Visuals** Transparencies 1 and 2a. Guide students to name regions of France and French-speaking countries. Encourage students to share what they have learned about France and the French-speaking world. Help summarize the diversity and extent of the French-speaking world. As an alternative, replay the **Video** before summarizing the cultural influence of France throughout the world.

❑ Invite local French speakers to visit the class to give personal opinions as to the value of knowing the French language, as described in MULTI-CULTURAL ENRICHMENT at the bottom of page T3.

UNITÉ 1, LEÇON 1: *La rentrée,* PAGE 14

Objectives

Communicative Functions and Topics	To say hello and ask someone's name
	To introduce oneself and spell one's name
	To talk about telephone numbers using 0–10
Linguistic Goals	To use *je/tu* and *moi/toi*
	To recognize spelling marks and accents
Cultural Goals	To compare greetings and interactions used in France and in the United States
	To recognize French first names

Note: Concentrate on listening and speaking skills in the lessons of *Niveau A*. Keep the pace moving and lively. The material will be recycled later in *Niveau B*.

Motivation and Focus

❑ Talk about French greeting customs using **Overhead Visuals** Transparency S3 and the photos on pages 10–13 of the text-book. Discuss similarities and differences between what students see here and how they greet each other. Read the *Introduction culturelle: Salutations* on page 12. Do the CROSS-CULTURAL OBSERVATION, page T13.

❑ Explain that the students in the photos are beginning a new school year after their summer vacation. Have students discuss how they feel on the first day of school.

❑ Begin **Interdisciplinary/Community Connections** Project One, pages 45–47.

Presentation and Explanation

❑ *Lesson Opener:* Model or play the **Audio** or **Video** for the mini-conversations on page 14. Replay with students reading along. Discuss what they think the people in the pictures are saying.

❑ *Pour communiquer:* Explain expressions in the box, page 15. Share the information in LANGUAGE NOTES on page T15. Do **Activity Book** exercises A–B, page 3.

❑ *Notes culturelles:* Have students read *La rentrée* and *Les prénoms français* on page 15. Guide students to find information on the sign in the photo and to develop cultural awareness using the CROSS-CULTURAL OBSERVATION, page T15.

❑ *Petit commentaire:* Read about **Astérix** on page 16; share information in the TE margin with them. Ask them to compare **Astérix** to one of their favorite cartoon characters.

❑ Introduce numbers 0–10; practice them using the SPEAKING ACTIVITY on page T17.

❑ *Les signes orthographiques:* Model and have students repeat the French alphabet. Ask students to spell their names in French. Point out accents and spelling marks in the box on page 17. Share the LANGUAGE NOTES in the margin on page T17.

Guided Practice and Checking Understanding

❑ Practice greetings using **Overhead Visuals** Transparencies S3 and S4 as cues and the suggestions on pages A7–A8. Follow the suggestions on page T15, having students choose French names and introduce themselves.

❑ Use the **Audio** or **Cassette Script** for **Activity Book** listening activities C–J, pages 3–5. Alternatively, play **Video** sections 1.1–1.3 and have students complete pages 1–4 of the **Video Activity Book**.

❑ Review numbers using the TPR activity on page T17.

Independent Practice

❏ Model and have students repeat activities 1–6, pages 16–17. Practice activitles 1–5 in pairs. Alternatively, have students work in threes: two students practicing the exchanges and the third checking their work in the **Answer Key**.

Monitoring and Adjusting

❏ Assign **Activity Book** Writing Activities 1–3, pages 19–20. Go over the answers with the class.
❏ Use the **Writing Template** for Unit 1 to monitor use of the expressions taught in this lesson.
❏ Practice the alphabet with the TEACHING THE ALPHABET strategy on page T16.
❏ Use **Teaching to Multiple Intelligences** activities 2–3 on pages 10–12 to review the alphabet and numbers.

Assessment

❏ Administer Quiz 1 on page 33 of **Lesson Quizzes** after all of the lesson's activities are completed. Use the **Test Bank** to create additional assessment activities.

Reteaching

❏ Play the **Video** to reteach greeting and to have the class practice the exchanges again.
❏ Individual students can use the **CD-ROM** to review portions of the lesson or for make-up work.
❏ Redo any activities in the **Activity Book** with which students had difficulty.

Extension and Enrichment

❏ To review the French alphabet and names of people and places that they have studied, play the GAME: LE PENDU on page T16.
❏ Assign research on *la jour de rentrée* or *Astérix* in **Internet Connection Notes** Internet Project 1 or 2 on pages 1–3.
❏ Individual students may use the **CD-ROM** for extension and enrichment.

Summary and Closure

❏ Ask pairs of students to demonstrate how to say hello, introduce themselves, ask someone's name, spell their names, and count to 10.
❏ Show **Overhead Visuals** Transparency S4 and invite pairs to role play the situations. You may wish to videotape some of the role plays for inclusion in the students' Oral Portfolios, which are described on pages 2–3 of **Portfolio Assessment**.

UNITÉ 1, LEÇON 2: *Tu es français?*, PAGE 18

Objectives

Communicative Functions and Topics	To say where you are from
	To talk about nationality
Linguistic Goals	To use masculine and feminine adjectives: ***français/française***
	To use *je suis* and *tu es*
	To count from 10 to 20
	To recognize silent letters at the end of words
Cultural Goals	To become more familiar with Martinique and its capital, Fort-de-France
	To understand the extent of French national territory

Motivation and Focus

❑ After reviewing greetings, ask students to look at the pictures on page 18. Point to each picture and ask, "***Français(e)?***" Answer with "***Oui***" or "***Non***," nodding or shaking your head. Then point to students in the class and ask "***Français(e)?***" Encourage students to answer "***Non.***"

❑ Have students identify the nationalities of the people on pages 2–3 in the previous Cultural Photo Essay or from **Video** section A.4.

❑ If students want to learn more about the French-speaking world, have them select the activity on page 47 in **Interdisciplinary/Community Connections**.

Presentation and Explanation

❑ *Lesson Opener:* With books closed, model or use the **Audio** to present the exchanges on page 18. Repeat, pausing to have students identify the nationalities. Then have students read the conversations; ask them to imagine what is being said.

❑ *Pour communiquer:* Use **Overhead Visuals** Transparency 4 to discuss nationalities. Introduce the expressions from the box on page 19, and point out the difference between masculine and feminine forms.

❑ *Note culturelle:* Ask students to read about Martinique on page 19. Encourage students to talk about who is French. Share the information from the CULTURAL NOTE, page T19. Play **Video** section 2.3, or read the **Video Script**.

❑ *Petit commentaire:* Have students read about the Statue of Liberty and Eiffel Tower on page 20. Discuss the information in the TE margin.

❑ Introduce numbers 10–20 and have students practice saying them.

❑ *Prononciation:* Model the words in the box on page 21. Point out final silent letters. Play **Audio** 2.3 and have students repeat.

Guided Practice and Checking Understanding

❑ Do the role play activity on page A52 of **Overhead Visuals** with Transparency 4.

❑ Check listening skills by using activities C–E on pages 7–8 of the **Activity Book** with the **Audio** or by reading the **Cassette Script**.

❑ Play the **Video** or read the **Video Script** while students do the activities on pages 5–7 of the **Video Activity Book**.

❑ Use the LISTENING COMPREHENSION ACTIVITY at the bottom of page T19 to practice adjective agreement, and the TPR activity on page T21 for numbers.

Independent Practice

❏ Model the activities on pages 20–21. Have students work in threes, with two students practicing the exchanges and the third using the **Answer Key** to check their work.

❏ Use **Communipak**, pages 3, 7–8, and 9, for Interview 1, Conversation 1, and Échange 1. For more group work with nationalities, use **Video Activity Book** activity 5, page 8.

Monitoring and Adjusting

❏ Monitor students' ability to talk about nationality and where they are from as they do the activities. Refer them to the expressions in *Pour communiquer* as needed.

❏ Have students do **Activity Book** Writing Activities 1–3, pages 21–22.

❏ To monitor students' use of nationalities and adjective agreement, follow the EXTRA SPEAKING ACTIVITY suggestions in the margin of page T20, and use **Teaching to Multiple Intelligences** activities 4–6 on pages 13–16.

❏ Use the **Writing Template** to monitor students' production of the lesson's content.

Assessment

❏ After students have completed all of the lesson's activities, administer Quiz 2 on page 34 of **Lesson Quizzes**. You may adapt the questions to your class's needs with the **Test Bank**.

Reteaching

❏ Redo any of the activities in the **Activity Book** with which students had difficulty.

❏ Students can review parts of the lesson with the **CD-ROM** or **Video**.

Extension and Enrichment

❏ Individual students can use the **CD-ROM** for extension and enrichment.

❏ To encourage students to note similarities and differences between French and American schools, do the COOPERATIVE LEARNING activity on page T18.

❏ Students may want to select one of the four **Internet Connection Notes** Internet Project 3 activities on pages 4–7.

Summary and Closure

❏ Have students work in pairs on Tu as la parole activities 1 and 5 on pages 5–6 in **Communipak**. Invite pairs to present their responses to the class. As a group, summarize the structures and expressions that students have learned in the lesson. You may wish to videotape students' presentation for inclusion in their Oral Portfolios.

UNITÉ 1, LEÇON 3: *Salut! Ça va?*, PAGE 22

Objectives

Communicative Functions and Topics
To greet friends/classmates and teachers/other adults appropriately

To ask how people feel

To express feelings of frustration and appreciation

To say good-bye

Linguistic Goals
To use expressions with *ça va*

To learn when to pronounce final consonants

Cultural Goals
To be aware of formal and casual greetings used in French

To become familiar with the use of *monsieur*, *madame*, and *mademoiselle* and their abbreviations

Motivation and Focus

❏ Introduce the lesson by using the suggestions in SETTING THE SCENE on TE page 22. Ask students to suggest ways of greeting and addressing people. Point out expressions and gestures used for friends, new acquaintances, teachers, and other adults.

❏ Show **Overhead Visuals** Transparency S4 and ask students to tell whether the people are in France or the United States; discuss how they know.

Presentation and Explanation

❏ *Lesson Opener:* Model or play the **Audio** and have students repeat the exchanges on page 22 as they follow along in their books. Have students read the exchanges on page 22 and try to guess what is being said.

❏ *Pour communiquer:* Use **Overhead Visuals** Transparency S4 to introduce formal and informal greetings. Point out the expressions in the box on page 23.

❏ *Note culturelle:* Read *Bonjour ou Salut?* on page 23; also play **Video** 3.3, or read the **Video Script**. Guide students to point out similarities and differences in greeting customs in France and in the U.S.

❏ *Pour communiquer:* Use **Overhead Visuals** Transparency 5 to introduce expressions with *ça va* from the box on page 22. Have students use the expressions to ask and tell how they are.

❏ Introduce numbers 20–60, page T25; have students repeat and practice.

❏ *Prononciation:* Explain and practice the pronunciation of final consonants on page 25. Use **Audio** 3.4 and have students repeat.

Guided Practice and Checking Understanding

❏ Use **Overhead Visuals** Transparencies S4 and 4, with the activities on pages A9 and A51–A52, to practice greetings and asking and telling how people feel.

❏ Play sections 3.1–3.3 of the **Audio**, or read the **Cassette Script**, as students do activities C–F on pages 11–13 of the **Activity Book**.

❏ Play the **Video**, or read the **Video Script**, as students do pages 9–11 of the **Video Activity Book**.

❏ Practice numbers with the TPR activity on page T25.

Independent Practice

- ❏ Model and have students repeat activities 1–4 on pages 24–25 as a class before having students practice in pairs.
- ❏ To practice greetings and numbers in pairs, use the following activities: **Communipak**, Tu as la parole 2–4 and 6, pages 5–6, Conversation 2, pages 7–8, and Tête à tête 1, pages 11–12, or **Video Activity Book**, page 12.

Monitoring and Adjusting

- ❏ Monitor students' work as they complete Writing Activities 1–4 in the **Activity Book**, pages 23–24. Go over the answers with the class.
- ❏ Monitor students' production as they do the activities. Follow the suggestions in the TE margins, and use the TEACHING STRATEGY on page T23 and the TEACHING NOTE on page T24.
- ❏ Do **Teaching to Multiple Intelligences** activity 8 on page 18 to practice numbers with a popular French melody. To monitor students' understanding of expressions for feelings, follow the suggestions on page 17 of **Teaching to Multiple Intelligences**.
- ❏ Use the **Writing Template** to monitor students' production of the lesson's vocabulary and structures.

Assessment

- ❏ Administer Quiz 3 on page 35 of **Lesson Quizzes** after students have completed all of the lesson's activities. Use the **Test Bank** to adapt quiz questions to your class's needs.

Reteaching

- ❏ Redo any appropriate activities from the **Activity Book**.
- ❏ Do **Teacher to Teacher** pages 2 and 3 to reteach and reinforce numbers 1–60.
- ❏ Have students use the **CD-ROM** or **Video** for review as needed.

Extension and Enrichment

- ❏ Individual students may use the **CD-ROM** for extension and enrichment.
- ❏ Students may choose to do one of the three activities listed on pages 8–9 of **Internet Connection Notes**. Encourage students to share their findings with the class.

Summary and Closure

- ❏ Invite students to present to the class any of the **Video Activity Book** or **Communipak** role plays. As a group, make a list of situations for using formal and informal greetings in French. Compare to American customs. Videotape or audiotape selected presentations for inclusion in students' Oral Portfolios.

UNITÉ 1, LEÇON 4: *L'heure,* PAGE 26

Objectives

Communicative Functions and Topics
To ask for and indicate the time, including hours, half hours, quarter hours, and minutes

To ask and say when certain events are scheduled

To talk about appointments or dates

Linguistic Goals
To use question expressions for time: *Quelle heure* and *À quelle heure*

To respond to questions about time: *Il est*, *À*

Cultural Goals
To learn about the French 24-hour clock system

Motivation and Focus

❏ Have students look at the photos on page 26 and suggest where the characters are and what time it is. Ask them to identify typical daily and weekend activities and corresponding times for the activities.

❏ Play section 4.5 of the **Video**, or read that section in the **Video Script**, page 9. Discuss *L'heure officielle*. Explain the CROSS-CULTURAL OBSERVATION, page T27. Ask students to think about places in the U.S. where the 24-hour time system is used.

Presentation and Explanation

❏ *Lesson Opener:* Use the WARM-UP activity on page T26 to review numbers. To present the opening conversation, model or play **Audio** 4.1. Replay with students reading along. Then discuss what they think the conversation is about.

❏ *Pour communiquer:* Introduce asking the time and telling time with **Overhead Visuals** Transparency 6. Discuss the information in the boxes on pages 26–28. Use **Audio** 4.3 or model conversation B on page 28. Then read and discuss it with the students. Present the information in the box on page 28.

Guided Practice and Checking Understanding

❏ Practice telling time using the Description on page A53 and the Goal 2 activity on page A54 of **Overhead Visuals**, and with the TPR activities on pages T27 and T28.

❏ Use the **Audio** or **Cassette Script** to do the listening activities in the **Activity Book**: C–D on page 15 and G–J on pages 16–17.

❏ Play the **Video** or read the **Video Script** as students do **Video Activity Book** activities 1–6, pages 13–15. Go over the answers with the class.

Independent Practice

❏ Model activities 1–5 on pages 27 and 29 before having students work in pairs to practice them. Use **Overhead Visuals** Transparency 1 to do the GEOGRAPHY SKILLS activity, page T29, before practicing asking and answering questions about train schedules in activity 6, page 29.

❏ Students can work on **Teacher to Teacher** page 4 to practice time expressions.

❏ Use any or all of Conversations 3–4, Échange 2, or Tête à tête 2 in **Communipak**, pages 7–8, 10, and 13–14. Arrange students in pairs or groups to practice and present their conversations to the class. Students can also work in pairs to practice talking about train schedules using **Video Activity Book** page 16.

Monitoring and Adjusting

❏ As students work on the activities on pages 27 and 29, monitor their use of time expressions. Refer them to the expressions and explanations in *Pour communiquer* on pages 26–28 as needed.

❏ Have students do **Activity Book** Writing Activities on pages 25–26.

❏ Use **Teaching to Multiple Intelligences** activity 9, pages 19–20, to model questions and answers about time.

❏ Monitor students' production of the content of the lesson with the **Writing Template**.

Assessment

❏ After students have completed the lesson, administer Quiz 4 on pages 37–38 of **Lesson Quizzes**. Use Unit Test 1 (Form A or B) on pages 23–28 of **Unit Tests** as a comprehensive check.

❏ Choose any or all of the **Proficiency Tests** for Unit 1 as alternative assessments. The **Test Bank** can be used to adapt tests to a class's specific needs.

Reteaching

❏ Redo activities in the **Activity Book** that correspond to language items that students may be finding difficult.

❏ Students can use the **CD-ROM** or **Video** to review portions of the lesson.

Extension and Enrichment

❏ Individual students may use the **CD-ROM** for extension and enrichment.

❏ Students can learn more about French schedules and tourist attractions with **Internet Connection Notes** activities 5A–C on pages 10–12. You may also introduce and begin the Long-Term Internet Project on page 13 if desired.

Summary and Closure

❏ Help students use the two dialogues in this lesson as models to create their own dialogues about time and appointments. Students can present the dialogues to the class, or they can be videotaped for inclusion in students' Oral Portfolios.

End-of-Unit Activities

Note: These activities may be done at the end of the unit, or at any time that seems appropriate during the unit.

❏ *À votre tour!:* Use the suggestions at the bottom and in the margins of pages T30–T31 to give students extra oral practice and to review the functions and structures introduced in this unit.

❏ *Entracte 1:* Have students look for cognates with the Pre-reading and Post-reading activities at the bottom of page T32. Use the suggestions in the TE margin to help students read and pronounce the signs. Discuss French influence in American place names with the selection on page 33. Explain the Cultural note on page T33, and follow the Pre-reading and Post-reading activities at the bottom of the page.

❏ *Reading and Culture Activities:* Encourage students to use their knowledge of cognates when doing the activities on pages 27–30 of the **Activity Book**.

UNITÉ 2, LEÇON 5: *Copain ou copine?*, PAGE 36

Objectives

Communicative Functions and Topics
To introduce or point out someone
To find out who someone is
To get someone's attention or to express surprise
To talk about people
To say telephone numbers using numbers 60 to 79

Linguistic Goals
To use *un (garçon)* and *une (fille)*
To use liaison to link words in French

Cultural Goals
To be aware of the French concept of friendship
To understand how different words can distinguish among different kinds of friends

Motivation and Focus

❑ Begin a discussion on friendship with the *Introduction culturelle* and photos on pages 34–35. Ask students to say what a good friend is, what activities they like to do with friends, and identify some of their friends. Encourage students to comment on the relationships pictured and compare them to American friendships.

❑ Talk about the CROSS-CULTURAL OBSERVATION and HISTORICAL NOTE on page T35.

❑ Do the SETTING THE STAGE activity about boys' and girls' names on page T36.

❑ If desired, begin the Family Celebrations project on pages 48–50 of **Interdisciplinary/Community Connections**.

Presentation and Explanation

❑ *Lesson Opener:* Model the conversations on page 36, or play the **Audio** or **Video**, and have students repeat the lines. Have students read the exchanges, and discuss what they think is being said.

❑ *Pour communiquer:* Introduce expressions used to point out someone and find out about someone, in the box on page 37, using **Overhead Visuals** Transparency 7. Model and have students repeat. Explain the LANGUAGE NOTE on page T37.

❑ *Note culturelle:* To present friendship terms in French, read the box on page 37. Point out the different forms used for boys and girls. You may also play **Video** 5.3, or read the **Video Script**. Explain the CULTURAL NOTE on page T37.

❑ *Petit commentaire:* Read the information about the Tour de France on page 38. Share the information in the TE margin with the students.

❑ *Grammar:* Call attention to and explain the use of *un* and *une* with masculine and feminine nouns in the grammar box on page 38.

❑ *Prononciation:* Use the box on page 39 to present and practice liaison between words. Play **Audio** 5.4 and have students repeat.

❑ Introduce and practice numbers 60–79 in the box on page 39.

Guided Practice and Checking Understanding

❑ Practice identifying people with **Overhead Visuals** Transparency 7 and the activities on pages A55 and A56.

❑ Use the **Audio** or **Cassette Script** with listening activities C–F in the **Activity Book**, pages 35–36.

❑ To check understanding, replay the **Video** for Module 5 or read the **Video Script**, and do pages 17–19 in the **Video Activity Book**.

❑ Use the TPR activity on page T37 to practice nouns and articles.

Independent Practice

- ❏ Do oral practice activities 1–4 on pages 38–39. Students can do activities 1 and 3 alone or for homework. Arrange students in threes to practice activities 2 and 4. Two students can role play the conversation while the third student checks their work in the **Answer Key**. Students can switch roles and practice again.

- ❏ To practice identifying friends, do **Communipak** Conversations 3–4, pages 23–24. As an alternative, students can compare lists of friends with **Video Activity Book** activity 5, page 20.

Monitoring and Adjusting

- ❏ Students can work individually on writing with **Activity Book** activities 1–4 on pages 47–48. Go over the answers with the class.

- ❏ As students work on activities, monitor use of articles. Refer students to the grammar box on page 38. Use the TEACHING NOTES on the bottom of page T38 to help students discriminate between the articles.

- ❏ Use **Teaching to Multiple Intelligences** activities 1 and 2, pages 21–22, to monitor students' understanding of vocabulary and numbers 60–79.

- ❏ Monitor students' production of the structures and vocabulary of this lesson with the **Writing Template**.

Assessment

- ❏ Administer Quiz 5 on pages 39–40 of **Lesson Quizzes** after completing all of the lesson's activities. The **Test Bank** can be used to adjust or create new quizzes.

Reteaching

- ❏ Redo any activities in the **Activity Book** that may cause students difficulty.
- ❏ Students can use the **CD-ROM** or **Video** to review portions of the lesson.

Extension and Enrichment

- ❏ Individual students can use the **CD-ROM** for extension and enrichment.
- ❏ Play the GAME: MINI-LOTO on page T39.
- ❏ If students are interested, have them do **Internet Connection Notes** Internet Project 1 on page 15. Encourage students to share information about their Internet penpals.

Summary and Closure

- ❏ Using **Overhead Visuals** Transparency S5 and the activities on pages A10–A11, have students demonstrate how to point out people, find out who someone is, and identify people. You may videotape selected presentations for students' Oral Portfolios.

UNITÉ 2, LEÇON 6: *Une coïncidence,* PAGE 40

Objectives

Communicative Functions and Topics
To find out another person's name
To describe people and give their nationalities
To inquire about people
To talk about area codes for French cities using numbers 80 to 100

Linguistic Goals
To use *le (garçon)* and *la (fille)*
To pronounce the nasal vowel /ɛ̃/

Cultural Goals
To be aware of the importance of French heritage in Quebec, Canada

Motivation and Focus

❏ Use **Overhead Visuals** Transparency 4 with the WARM-UP AND REVIEW activity about nationalities on page T40.

❏ Have students look at the photos on page 41 of the textbook and describe the city scenes. Encourage them to compare the cities in the photos to their local town or city.

❏ Play the Vignette culturelle, section 6.3 of the **Video**, or read the **Video Script**, pointing out sights and views of Quebec and Montreal for discussion. Students can share information about any travel experiences they have had in Quebec and Montreal.

Presentation and Explanation

❏ *Lesson Opener:* Model the opening conversation, or play the **Video** or **Audio**, section 6.1. Have students read the exchanges and guess what the people are talking about.

❏ *Pour communiquer:* With books open to page 41, introduce the expressions in the box. Have students repeat and use the expressions to ask and talk about others in the class.

❏ *Note culturelle:* Read *Montréal et la province de Québec* on page 41. Guide discussion of the importance of French language and culture in the eastern part of Canada. Share the information in the PHOTO CULTURE NOTES, page T41.

❏ *Petit commentaire:* Have students read the top of page 42. They can talk about local places and information they would share with a French exchange student.

❏ *Grammar:* Briefly point out the masculine and feminine forms of "the" in the grammar box on page 42.

❏ After you introduce numbers 80–100, explain the LANGUAGE and PRONUNCIATION notes on page T43.

❏ *Prononciation:* Point out the box on page 43 and have students practice saying the nasal vowel sounds as you model or use **Audio** 6.4.

❏ Try to move quickly through the lesson, focusing on listening and speaking skills.

Guided Practice and Checking Understanding

❏ Use **Overhead Visuals** Transparency 7 and the activities on pages A55–A56 to have students practice asking names.

❏ Have students do **Activity Book** activities C–F on pages 37–38 as they listen to the **Audio**, or listen as you read the **Cassette Script**.

❏ Use pages 21–23 in the **Video Activity Book** to check students' listening skills as they watch the **Video** or listen as you read the **Video Script**.

❏ Use **Overhead Visuals** Transparency 7 to do the TPR activity on page T42.

Independent Practice

❏ Model the activities on pages 42–43. Do 1 and 4 for homework. Students can practice activities 2 and 3 in pairs and check their work with the **Answer Key**.

❏ Arrange students in pairs to practice using numbers with **Communipak** Tu as la parole 3 and 4, page 22. Have students work in groups identifying famous people in the **Video Activity Book**, page 24.

Monitoring and Adjusting

❏ Monitor students' use of the lesson expressions and structures as they work on the activities. Remind students to study *Pour communiquer* on page 41 and the grammar box on page 42 as needed.

❏ Assign Writing Activities 1–4 on pages 49–50 in the **Activity Book**.

❏ If students need additional help with numbers, use **Teaching to Multiple Intelligences** activity 3 on page 23.

Assessment

❏ After completing the lesson, use Quiz 6 on pages 41–42 of **Lesson Quizzes**. The **Test Bank** can be used to adjust the quiz to meet the class's particular needs.

Reteaching

❏ Redo any activities in the **Activity Book** that need to be retaught.

❏ Use the **CD-ROM** or **Video** to have students review portions of the lesson.

❏ Use EXPANSION suggestions on page T42 for exercise 2, to reteach identifying people.

Extension and Enrichment

❏ Individual students can use the **CD-ROM** for expansion and enrichment.

❏ Students can learn about French celebrities with **Internet Connection Notes** Internet Project 2 on page 16.

❏ Students can locate the French cities in exercise 5, page 43, on the map of France shown on **Overhead Visuals** Transparency 2. Follow the teaching tips for MAP WORK, page T43, and explain the information in the CULTURAL NOTES.

❏ Have students practice numbers by playing the GAME: NUMBERS 11 TO 99 on page T43.

Summary and Closure

❏ Ask pairs of students to prepare mini-dialogues in which they ask about someone, find out that person's name, and describe the person's nationality. Have them present the dialogues to the class. You may videotape them for students' Oral Portfolios.

UNITÉ 2, LEÇON 7: *Les photos d'Isabelle*, PAGE 44

Objectives

Communicative Functions and Topics
To find out how old a friend is
To ask about how old others are
To introduce and talk about family members

Linguistic Goals
To use *mon (cousin)* and *ma (cousine)*; *ton (cousin)* and *ta (cousine)*
To pronounce the nasal vowels /ã/ and /ɔ̃/

Cultural Goals
To compare French and American concepts of the family

Motivation and Focus

❏ Encourage students to compare French and American families by playing **Video** 7.4 or reading the **Video Script**. Do the CROSS-CULTURAL OBSERVATION on page T45.

❏ Invite students to talk about the different relationships represented in their families. Ask them to look at the photos on page 44 and suggest what family members are pictured.

Presentation and Explanation

❏ *Lesson Opener:* To introduce the lesson, use the WARM-UP AND REVIEW activity on page T44 to identify students in the class. Play the **Video** or **Audio** 7.1 to present the lesson, or model the opening monologue. Ask students to read page 44 and discuss what they think is being said.

❏ *Pour communiquer:* Introduce family relationship terms using **Overhead Visuals** Transparency 8. Point out the expressions in the box on page 45.

❏ *Note culturelle:* Read *La famille français* on page 45. Discuss differences and similarities between French and American families.

❏ *Petit commentaire:* Read about pets at the top of page 46, and discuss the notes in the TE margins.

❏ *Grammar:* Briefly explain adjective agreement using the grammar box on page 46 and the TEACHING NOTES in the TE margin.

❏ *Pour communiquer:* Use the WARM-UP AND REVIEW activity on page T46 to review numbers before introducing questions and answers about age in the box on page 47.

❏ *Prononciation:* Model and have students practice nasal vowels with the box on page 47. Play **Audio** 7.4. Have students repeat.

Guided Practice and Checking Understanding

❏ Have students practice introducing family members with **Overhead Visuals** Transparency 8 and the activities on pages A57 and A58.

❏ Play the **Audio**, or read the **Cassette Script**, and have students do **Activity Book** activities C–F on pages 40–42.

❏ To check understanding of the lesson, use the **Video** or **Video Script** with activities 1–4 on pages 25–28 in the **Video Activity Book**.

❏ Practice family vocabulary with the TPR activity on page T45.

Independent Practice

❏ Do the activities on pages 46–47. Assign activity 1 for homework. Go over the answers with the class. Model and have students repeat activities 2–5 before having students practice in pairs, checking their answers in the **Answer Key**.

❏ Do any of the following: **Communipak** Tu as la parole 1 and 2, Conversation 2, Échanges 2 and 3, or Tête à tête 1 and 2 (pages 21–32), or **Video Activity Book** activity 5, page 28, for pair practice asking and answering questions about family members and ages.

Monitoring and Adjusting

❏ Assign Writing Activities 1–4 in the **Activity Book**, pages 51–52, for students to work on individually. Go over the answers with the class.

❏ Monitor students' use of age expressions, family vocabulary, and adjective agreement as they work on the practice activities. Refer them to the grammar and vocabulary boxes as needed. Use the TEACHING NOTES on page T46 and the TEACHING STRATEGY: AGES on page T47.

❏ Use activity 4 on pages 24–27 of **Teaching to Multiple Intelligences** to practice vocabulary related to family members and numbers.

❏ Monitor students' writing with the **Writing Template**.

Assessment

❏ Have students take Quiz 7 on pages 43–44 of **Lesson Quizzes** after all of the lesson's activities are completed. Use the **Test Bank** to adapt questions to your needs.

Reteaching

❏ If students are having difficulty with any of the lesson's structures or vocabulary, have them redo the corresponding activities in the **Activity Book**.

❏ Students can use the **CD-ROM** or **Video** to review portions of the lesson.

Extension and Enrichment

❏ Individual students can use the **CD-ROM** for extension and enrichment.

❏ Use the SUPPLEMENTARY VOCABULARY list on page T45 to introduce additional family relationship terms to challenge more advanced students.

❏ If students are interested, have them do **Internet Connection Notes** Internet Project 3, page 17, to create a family website.

Summary and Closure

❏ Use **Overhead Visuals** Transparency S6 and the activities on page A12 to have students present role plays in which they introduce and talk about family members, and ask about how old people are. You may videotape selected presentations for inclusion in students' Oral Portfolios.

UNITÉ 2, LEÇON 8: *Le jour et la date,* PAGE 48

Objectives

Communicative Functions To talk about days of the week
and Topics To tell people when you will see them again
To talk about the date
To talk about birthdays
Linguistic Goals To express a date in French
To use casual question forms: *C'est quand?*
Cultural Goals To compare date patterns in French and English

Motivation and Focus

❏ Have students share birthdays to prepare them for the focus of the lesson.
❏ Play **Video** 8.3, Joyeux anniversaire!, or read the **Video Script**. Discuss students' impressions of French birthday celebrations.

Presentation and Explanation

❏ *Lesson Opener:* Use the WARM-UP AND REVIEW activity on page T48 to provide practice with expressing feelings. Model or present dialogues A and B with **Video** or **Audio** 8.1. Pause to encourage student comments on the conversations and situations. Have students read the conversations and discuss what is being said.
❏ *Pour communiquer:* Introduce and practice days of the week and the expressions in the box on page 49 with **Overhead Visuals** Transparency 9. Explain the CULTURAL NOTE in the margin of page T49. Present months of the year and expressions for talking about dates in *Pour communiquer* on page 50 with the same transparency. Explain the pattern used in French to express dates, as presented in the grammar box on page 51.

Guided Practice and Checking Understanding

❏ Practice talking about days and dates with **Overhead Visuals** Transparency 9. Discuss the French calendar with the Goal 2 activity on page A59.
❏ To check understanding, use the **Audio** or the **Cassette Script** and **Activity Book** activities C–H, pages 43–45.
❏ Play the **Video**, or read the **Video Script**, as students do pages 29–31 in the **Video Activity Book**.

Independent Practice

❏ Model and have students repeat the practice activities on pages 49 and 51. Activities 1, 2, 3, and 6 can be done for homework and 4 and 5 in pairs, with students checking their answers in the **Answer Key**.
❏ Arrange students in pairs to practice asking and answering questions about birthdays and dates with **Communipak** Interviews 1–4, Conversation 1, Échange 1, or Tête à tête 3 (pages 19–34), or **Video Activity Book** Activité 6, page 32.

Monitoring and Adjusting

❏ Have students work on Writing Activities 1–4 on pages 53–54 in the **Activity Book**.
❏ Monitor students' understanding as they work on the practice activities. Have them study the expressions and vocabulary in the *Pour communiquer* boxes on pages 49–50 and the grammar box on page 51.

❏ Monitor students' comprehension of days and dates as they work with **Teaching to Multiple Intelligences** activities 5 and 6 on pages 28–33.

Assessment

❏ Use Quiz 8 on pages 45–46 of **Lesson Quizzes** after students have completed the lesson. Administer Unit Test 2 (Form A or B) on pages 29–36 of **Unit Tests** as a comprehensive assessment of the unit's goals and objectives. Choose any or all of the **Proficiency Tests** as needed for additional assessment. The **Test Bank** can be used to modify tests and quizzes or create new ones to fit the class's needs and situation.

Reteaching

❏ Have students redo any of the **Activity Book** activities with which they had difficulty.

❏ Reteach birthdays, days, and dates using either of the following: VARIATION activity 4, page T51, or **Teacher to Teacher**, page 5.

❏ Assign the **CD-ROM** or **Video** for students who need review.

Extension and Enrichment

❏ Individual students can use the **CD-ROM** for extension and enrichment.

❏ If students are interested, have them complete **Internet Connection Notes** Internet Project 4 on page 18, or the long-term project on page 19.

Summary and Closure

❏ As a culminating activity, review grammar and culture for *Unit 2* by having students play the game *La Tour Eiffel* on pages 34–42 of **Teaching to Multiple Intelligences**. Point out vocabulary and cultural information that students have learned.

End-of-Unit Activities

Note: These activities may be done at the end of the unit, or at any appropriate time during the unit.

❏ *À votre tour!:* Students can work in pairs on any or all of activities 1–5 on page 52. Students can check their own work on activities 1–3 using the **Audio** or **Cassette Script** for AVT2, or the **Answer Key**.

❏ *Entracte 2:* Do the PRE-READING and POST-READING ACTIVITIES on pages T54 and T55 to guide students through the readings. Discuss the PHOTO CULTURE NOTES on page T54 and use the TEACHING HINT on page T55.

❏ *Reading and Culture Activities:* Assign the activities on pages 55–58 of the **Activity Book**.

UNITÉ 3, LEÇON 9: *Tu as faim?*, PAGE 58

Objectives

Communicative Functions and Topics
To say you are hungry
To offer a friend something
To ask a friend for something
To talk about foods

Linguistic Goals
To use *un (sandwich)* and *une (pizza)* to understand masculine and feminine nouns
To recognize and repeat intonation

Cultural Goals
To become aware of what kinds of fast foods French young people buy

Motivation and Focus

❑ To introduce the unit, have students look at the opener on pages 56–57. Ask them to suggest what types of food might be served at the places in the pictures. Encourage students to share prior knowledge of *cafés* and *boulangeries*. Read aloud the *Introduction culturelle*. Discuss the information in the PHOTO CULTURE NOTES and LANGUAGE NOTES on page T57.

❑ Play **Video** 9.3 or read the **Video Script** for Qu'est-ce qu'on mange?. Explain the CULTURAL NOTE and do the CROSS-CULTURAL OBSERVATION, page T59.

❑ Present the project on pages 51–53 of **Interdisciplinary/Community Connections**. Arrange students in groups and help them begin to plan their projects.

Presentation and Explanation

❑ *Lesson Opener:* To present the opening conversations, model or play the **Video** or **Audio**. Then have students read the conversations; ask them to imagine what is being said. Share the information in the PHOTO CULTURE NOTE on page T58.

❑ *Pour communiquer:* Use **Overhead Visuals** Transparency 10 to present the food names and expressions in the box on page 59. Do the CROSS-CULTURAL OBSERVATION activity about food names on page T58. Use the questions to guide students' comments on the French food names.

❑ *Note culturelle:* Have students read *Les jeunes et la nourriture* on page 59. Discuss differences and similarities between what French teenagers and American teenagers eat.

❑ *Petit commentaire:* Read about French sandwiches on page 60. Share the additional information in the TE margin. Students may want to compare other American and French food items such as bread.

❑ *Grammar:* Briefly explain masculine and feminine articles and nouns in the grammar box, page 60. Revisit Transparency 10 to reinforce article and noun agreement.

❑ *Prononciation:* Point out intonation patterns in the box, page 61. Play **Audio** 9.4 and have students repeat.

Guided Practice and Checking Understanding

❑ Practice food vocabulary with **Overhead Visuals** Transparency 10.

❑ To check understanding, have students do **Activity Book** activities C–F on pages 63–64 as they listen to the **Audio** or **Cassette Script**.

❑ Play the **Video** or read the **Video Script** and have students do pages 33–35 in the **Video Activity Book**.

❑ Model and reinforce students' listening skills with the TPR activity, page T59.

Independent Practice

❏ Have students practice ordering food with the activities on pages 60–61. Activities 2 and 4 can be completed for homework. Model activities 1 and 3 before having students practice the dialogues in pairs. Students can check their own work with the **Answer Key**.

❏ Have students work in small groups to do activity 5 on page 36 of the **Video Activity Book**.

Monitoring and Adjusting

❏ Students can do Writing Activities 1–3 on pages 73–74 of the **Activity Book**.

❏ As students work on the whole-class and pair activities, monitor pronunciation and use of articles **un** and **une**. Refer students to grammar and intonation boxes on pages 60–61. Use SOUNDING FRENCH on page T61.

❏ Use **Teaching to Multiple Intelligences** activities 1 and 2, pages 43–46, to monitor food vocabulary and intonation.

❏ You may use the **Writing Template** to monitor students' written production of the structures and vocabulary of the lesson.

Assessment

❏ Administer Quiz 9 on pages 47–48 of **Lesson Quizzes** after students have completed all of the lesson's activities. Use the **Test Bank** to adjust the lesson quiz to the class's needs.

Reteaching

❏ Help students redo any activities in the **Activity Book** with which they had difficulty.

❏ Students can use the **CD-ROM** or **Video** to review portions of the lesson.

❏ Reteach masculine and feminine nouns with the LISTENING PRACTICE activity at the bottom of page T60.

Extension and Enrichment

❏ Individual students can use the **CD-ROM** for extension and enrichment.

❏ If students are interested, have them do **Internet Connection Notes** Internet Project 1 on page 21 about French cafés and restaurants.

Summary and Closure

❏ Use **Overhead Visuals** Transparency S7 and the activities on page A14 to have students demonstrate talking about foods, asking if someone is hungry, and asking for something. You may videotape the demonstrations for inclusion in students' Oral Portfolios.

UNITÉ 3, LEÇON 10: *Au café*, PAGE 62

Objectives

Communicative Functions and Topics
To identify beverages
To say that you are thirsty
To order a beverage in a café
To request something from a friend and from an adult

Linguistic Goals To use *s'il te plaît* and *s'il vous plaît*
To stress final syllables of words or groups of words

Cultural Goals To learn about *le café*

Motivation and Focus

❏ Ask students to look at the photos on pages 62–63; encourage them to describe the places and make comparisons to their own favorite eating places. Discuss with the class favorite beverages and places to go to get something to drink.

❏ Show the **Video** or read the **Video Script** for section 10.3. Point out the information in the PHOTO CULTURE NOTE and do CROSS-CULTURAL OBSERVATION, page T63, to compare French and American eating and drinking preferences.

Presentation and Explanation

❏ *Lesson Opener:* Do the WARM-UP AND REVIEW activity, page T62, to review forms of address. Act out or present the opening conversations with **Video** or **Audio** 10.1. Have students read page 62 and discuss what they think the conversation is about. Explain the LANGUAGE NOTES and the PHOTO CULTURE NOTE on page T62.

❏ *Pour communiquer:* Present the expressions and explain the two forms for "please" in the box on page 63.

❏ *Note culturelle:* Have students read *Le café* on page 63. Discuss similarities and differences in what French and American young people like to drink.

❏ *Petit commentaire:* Ask students to read the box on page 64 to find out about favorite beverages of French young people. Share the information in the TE margin. Encourage students to make comparisons to favorite American beverages.

❏ *Prononciation:* Explain French rhythm and stress patterns using the box on page 65. Guide students to accent the final syllable of a word or group of words. Use **Audio** 10.5 to model pronunciation; have students repeat.

Guided Practice and Checking Understanding

❏ Practice expressions related to beverages with **Overhead Visuals** Transparency 11 and the Goal 1 activity on page A61.

❏ Have students do **Activity Book** activities C–F on pages 66–67 for listening practice as you play the **Audio** or read the **Cassette Script**.

❏ Play the **Video** or read the **Video Script** as students do **Video Activity Book** pages 37–39.

❏ Practice beverage vocabulary with the TPR activity on page T63.

Independent Practice

❏ Model the activities on pages 64–65 and have students practice on their own or in pairs. Assign activity 3 for homework. Arrange students in pairs to practice the exchanges in activities 1–2 and 4. Have them check their own work with the **Answer Key**. Share the LANGUAGE NOTE, page T65, if desired.

❏ Use **Communipak** Interview 1, page 39, Conversations 1–2, pages 43–44, or Échange 1, page 45, for additional pair practice in ordering and requesting something. Use the **Video Activity Book**, page 40, for small group role plays of a scene at a café with a waiter/waitress taking customers' orders.

Monitoring and Adjusting

❏ Have students do **Activity Book** Writing Activities 1–3 on pages 75–76. Go over the answers with the class.

❏ Monitor students' language and pronunciation as they work on the activities on pages 64–65. Have them study the expressions and vocabulary in *Pour communiquer*, page 63, as needed. Use SOUNDING FRENCH on page T65.

❏ Monitor students' understanding of beverage vocabulary by using **Teaching to Multiple Intelligences** activity 3 on pages 47–48.

❏ Use the **Writing Template** to monitor students' written production.

Assessment

❏ After students have completed all of the lesson's activities, use Quiz 10 on pages 49–50 of **Lesson Quizzes**. Use the **Test Bank** to create additional assessment tools geared to the class's or individual students' needs.

Reteaching

❏ Reteach portions of the lesson as needed by redoing activities from the **Activity Book**.

❏ Students can use the **CD-ROM** or **Video** to review portions of the lesson.

Extension and Enrichment

❏ Individual students can use the **CD-ROM** for extension and enrichment.

❏ Play the GAME: C'EST LOGIQUE? on page T64.

❏ Students can learn about French soft drinks and beverage manufacturers with **Internet Connection Notes** Internet Project 2 on page 22.

Summary and Closure

❏ Have students demonstrate ordering food and beverages with **Overhead Visual** Transparency S8 and the activities on page A16. If desired, videotape the demonstrations for inclusion in students' Oral Portfolios. Guide students to summarize language expressions used for ordering food and to comment on similarities and differences between French cafés and students' favorite snack places.

UNITÉ 3, LEÇON 11: *Ça fait combien?*, PAGE 66

Objectives

Communicative Functions and Topics
To talk about menu items
To ask how much something costs
To ask a friend to lend you something

Linguistic Goals
To use *il* and *elle* to replace subject nouns
To pronounce the consonant "r"

Cultural Goals
To learn about the French monetary system

Motivation and Focus

❏ Ask students to look for numbers and words they know on the French money pictured on pages 66–67. Encourage students to point out the different denominations on the banknotes. Share the information in the CULTURAL NOTE, page T67.

❏ Play **Video** 11.3, or read the **Video Script**. Guide students to compare French and American monetary systems.

Presentation and Explanation

❏ *Lesson Opener:* Use the WARM-UP activity on page T66 to review numbers and practice addition problems. Model and act out the conversation, using gestures and expression to clarify meaning, or play **Audio** or **Video** 11.1. Ask students to read the conversation and summarize it.

❏ *Note culturelle:* Have students read *L'argent français* on pages 66–67. Share the information in the REALIA NOTE on page T67.

❏ *Pour communiquer:* Present expressions found in the box on page 67 for asking the price and asking a friend to lend money. Use the menu on **Overhead Visuals** Transparency 12 to cue questions about food prices. Point out casual speech forms in the LANGUAGE NOTE, page T67.

❏ *Petit commentaire:* Have students read the box on page 68 to learn about types of French restaurants. Share the information in the TE margin about the **Guide Michelin**.

❏ *Prononciation:* Explain how "r" is pronounced in French using the box on page 69. Use **Audio** section 11.4 for practice.

Guided Practice and Checking Understanding

❏ Have students practice asking how much something costs with **Overhead Visuals** Transparencies 10 and 11 and the REVIEW AND PRACTICE activities on pages A60–A61.

❏ Check students' listening comprehension with the **Audio** or **Cassette Script** with **Activity Book** activities C–D, pages 69–70.

❏ Play the **Video** or read the **Video Script** as students do **Video Activity Book** pages 41–43.

Independent Practice

❏ Do the activities on pages 68–69. Activity 1 can be done for homework. Arrange students in groups of three to practice activities 2 and 3. Have two students in each group practice the exchanges while the third student checks their work in the **Answer Key**. Students can switch roles and practice again. Have students work in pairs to prepare and present role plays for activity 4, page 69.

❏ For pair practice with asking and answering questions about the cost of food and beverages, use **Communipak** Tu as la parole 1–2, Conversation 3, or Tête à tête 1 (pages 41–48). In groups of two or three, have students use page 44 of the **Video Activity Book** to role play customers ordering at a restaurant and asking about prices of menu items.

Monitoring and Adjusting

❑ Have students work with **Activity Book** Writing Activities 1–2, pages 77–78.

❑ Monitor students' use of the structures and expressions introduced in this lesson, as well as pronunciation. Refer them to the information in the *Pour communiquer* box on page 67 as needed. If students have difficulty pronouncing "r," use the suggestions in the PRONUNCIATION note, page T69.

❑ Use activities 4 and 5 on pages 49–51 of **Teaching to Multiple Intelligences** to monitor students' ability to order foods and beverages and ask about prices.

❑ Monitor students' production of the language in this lesson with the **Writing Template**.

Assessment

❑ Administer Quiz 11 on pages 51–52 of **Lesson Quizzes** after the lesson's activities are completed. Use the **Test Bank** to adapt questions to your particular needs.

Reteaching

❑ Ask students to redo those activities in the **Activity Book** that correspond to language items with which they are having difficulty.

❑ Students can use the **CD-ROM** or **Video** to review portions of the lesson.

Extension and Enrichment

❑ Individual students may use the **CD-ROM** for extension and enrichment.

❑ Students can have extra practice with prices and menus using the GAME on page T67. They may want to prepare their own menus as described in PROJECT, page T68.

❑ Students can explore current exchange rates and practice converting French and American currency with **Internet Connection Notes** Internet Project 3, page 23.

Summary and Closure

❑ Use the activities on page A62 of **Overhead Visuals** with Transparency 12 to have students role play ordering in a restaurant and comparing French and American menu items. You may want to videotape selected role plays for inclusion in students' Oral Portfolios.

UNITÉ 3, LEÇON 12: *Le temps,* PAGE 70

Objectives

Communicative Functions and Topics
To talk about the weather
To use weather expressions
To identify seasons

Linguistic Goals To use *il fait* to talk about weather

Cultural Goals To learn about climates in various regions of France

Motivation and Focus

❏ Have students look at the map of France on page 6 and do the GEOGRAPHY activity and PRE-VIEWING activity, page T71. Play the **Video** or read the **Video Script** for section 12.3 to introduce the climate of the different provinces, using the map on **Overhead Visuals** Transparency 1.

Presentation and Explanation

❏ *Lesson Opener:* Use the WARM-UP AND REVIEW activity on page T70 to practice months and dates. With books closed, act out or use **Video** or **Audio** section 12.1 to present the opening conversation. Ask students to read and summarize the conversation.

❏ *Pour communiquer:* Introduce and practice describing weather conditions with **Overhead Visuals** Transparency 13. Point out and have students repeat the expressions and names of the seasons in the *Pour communiquer* box, page 71.

Guided Practice and Checking Understanding

❏ Use **Overhead Visuals** Transparency 13 and the activity on page A63 to practice weather expressions.

❏ To check understanding, use the **Audio** or read the **Cassette Script** as students do **Activity Book** activities C–D, pages 71–72.

❏ Play the **Video** or read the **Video Script** and have students do **Video Activity Book** pages 45–47.

❏ Practice weather expressions using the TPR activity on page T71.

Independent Practice

❏ Have students do activities 1 and 2 on page 71 individually and check their answers in the **Answer Key**.

❏ Use any of the following activities for pair practice in talking about the weather: **Communipak** Interview 2, Tu as la parole 3 and 4, Conversation 3, Échange 2, or Tête à tête 2 (pages 40–50); or **Video Activity Book** page 48.

Monitoring and Adjusting

❏ Assign **Activity Book** activities 1–4, pages 79–80, for writing practice.

❏ Monitor students' use of weather expressions as they do the practice activities. Remind them to look at the *Pour communiquer* box on page 71 of the text as needed.

❏ Use **Teaching to Multiple Intelligences** activities 6 and 7 on pages 52–54 to monitor students' use of seasons and weather terms.

Assessment

❏ Use Quiz 12 on pages 53–54 of **Lesson Quizzes** after students have completed the lesson. Unit Test 3 (Form A or B) on pages 37–42 of **Unit Tests** can be used as a comprehensive assessment of the unit's goals and objectives. Choose any or all of the **Proficiency Tests** as needed for additional assessment of specific language skills. The **Test Bank** can be used to modify test questions to meet your particular needs.

Reteaching

❏ Have students redo any appropriate activities in the **Activity Book**.

❏ Reteach weather expressions using **Teacher to Teacher** page 6.

❏ Assign the **CD-ROM** or **Video** for students who need to do review or make-up work.

Extension and Enrichment

❏ Individual students may use the **CD-ROM** for extension and enrichment.

❏ Students can do **Internet Connection Notes** Internet Project 4 on current European weather, page 24, or the Long-Term Internet Project on pages 25–26.

Summary and Closure

❏ Show **Overhead Visuals** Transparency 1 and ask students to point out and talk about the climate of the regions of France that were studied in the lesson. Summarize information about the climate of French geographical regions and weather conditions.

End-of-Unit Activities

Note: These activities may be done at the end of the unit, or at any appropriate time during the unit.

❏ *À votre tour!:* Choose any or all of the activities on pages 72–73. Students can use the **Audio** to check their responses for activities 1–3. Arrange students in pairs to practice and present the role plays in activities 4–5. Activity 6 can be done as a whole-class activity. Use the CHALLENGE ACTIVITY on page T73 to practice using language from this and previous units.

❏ *Entracte 3:* Introduce the song **Alouette** with the PRE-READING ACTIVITY on page T74. Share the cultural note with the class, sing the song, and do the POST-READING ACTIVITY. Introduce parts of the body with the TPR activity on page T75. Read *Un jeu* on page 75 and play the game. You may also wish to play the GAME described in the margin on page T75.

❏ *Reading and Culture Activities:* Assign **Activity Book** activities A–C, pages 81–83. Go over the answers with the class.

CULTURAL PHOTO ESSAY: *À l'école en France*, PAGE 76

Objectives

Cultural Goals   To learn about the French school system: grade levels and grading system

To compare typical French and American class days

To learn about French courses of study: subjects, schedule

To compare classrooms and buildings

Note: This Cultural Photo Essay presents information about the French school system and challenges students to compare their own school experiences in the U.S. to those of a typical student in France. You may want to refer back to this essay as students study more language for daily activities and communicating with friends.

Motivation and Focus

❑ As students preview the photos on pages 76–78 and 80, ask them to describe the scenes and suggest what a school day in France is like. Who are the people? Where are they? What are they doing? Together, read the photo captions on pages 77–78 and 80.

❑ Encourage students to describe their school and to talk about their favorite classes.

❑ As an overview of *À l'école en France*, play the **Video** or **Videodisc** sections B.1–B.4. Pause occasionally to allow students to comment on people and places.

Presentation and Explanation

❑ Together, read the letter and information about Nathalie on pages 76–77. Guide students to notice information about her family and home. Help students pronounce the names of Nathalie's school and town. Point out the information in the PHOTO CULTURE NOTE on page T77.

❑ Have students look at page 78. Encourage them to guess where the people are and what they are doing. Guide students as they look at the class schedule on page 79, noting days and times. Ask students to read *Un jour de classe* and *L'emploi du temps*. Explain the information in the *Note culturelle* and model the names of the school subjects.

❑ Present the information about French schools and grade levels on pages 80–81. Point out the floor plan of the school building in the background on page 80. Encourage students to comment on classroom set-up. Ask students how they might feel in the French classroom pictured on page 80. Discuss the chart in *Notes culturelles*, page 81. Guide students to notice differences in identifying class levels in the French and American school systems. Point out French names for schools. Have students read pages 80–81, assisting with pronunciation as needed.

❑ Use **Overhead Visuals** Transparency 50 to present classroom objects. Model the names of objects and have students repeat. Students can point to or find the objects in the rooms as you name them.

Guided Practice and Checking Understanding

❑ Have students try to identify the classes listed in the *Note culturelle*, page 79. Then guide students to talk about what subjects they take now.

❑ Use the TPR: CLASSROOM OBJECTS suggestions on page T83 to practice listening and following simple classroom directions with the objects on page 83. Students do not need to read and write the expressions on page 82; the focus is on comprehension. Help students use the ***Tu dis...*** expressions on page 83 to ask questions and talk about what they do and do not understand.

Independent Practice

❏ Students can work in small groups to compare French and American schools with the COOPERATIVE LEARNING activity on page T77. Invite groups to share their lists.

❏ When students answer the questions in *Activités culturelles*, pages 79 and 81, encourage them to use cognates and context clues as they look for information on the class schedule and report card.

Monitoring and Adjusting

❏ Monitor students' understanding of the French school system as they share their responses to the *Activités culturelles*. Clarify information as needed.

❏ Monitor students' comprehension of cultural similarities and differences between French and American school systems with activity 8 in **Teaching to Multiple Intelligences**, pages 55–56.

Assessment

❏ Use students' responses to *Activités culturelles* as an informal assessment of their awareness of cultural differences.

❏ To assess understanding of classroom objects, show **Overhead Visuals** Transparency S5. Invite students to point to objects as you say them.

Reteaching

❏ Use **Overhead Visuals** Transparency 50 to reteach names of classroom objects; then follow the instructions for the vocabulary game on page A125.

Extension and Enrichment

❏ Use **Overhead Visuals** Transparency S1 to introduce the SUPPLEMENTARY VOCABULARY on page T83. Then have students find the objects in the classroom scene on Transparency S2.

❏ Have students note the way times are written on Nathalie's class schedule. Students may want to rewrite their class schedules using the 24-hour system. If students are interested, have them find examples of schedules or situations where times are written in similar fashion in the U.S. Some examples might be transportation schedules or military times.

❏ Share the CULTURAL BACKGROUND information about *Le baccalauréat* on page T80. Encourage students to discuss or debate the pros and cons of the French school system. Students may want to consider Saturday classes, number of subjects studied, the grading system, and the *baccalauréat* test. Students should support their opinions.

Summary and Closure

❏ Show **Overhead Visuals** Transparency S5. Ask students to pretend they are one of the students in the picture and talk about their school life. Encourage them to share what they have learned about the French school system.

UNITÉ 4, LEÇON 13: *Mes activités*, PAGE 88

Objectives

Communicative Functions and Topics
To describe daily activities

To say what people do and don't do

To talk about what you want, would like, and do not want or like to do

To invite a friend, accept an invitation, and turn down an invitation

Linguistic Goals To use *je (veux)* and *je ne (veux) pas*

Cultural Goals To learn about daily activities of French young people

Motivation and Focus

❏ Have students look at the pictures on pages 84–87 and tell where the people in the photos are and what they are doing. Discuss similarities and differences between French and American activities. Use the CROSS-CULTURAL OBSERVATION and PHOTO CULTURE NOTE, page T87. Read *Thème et Objectifs* to preview the content of the unit.

❏ Students may begin Project Four on pages 54–57 of **Interdisciplinary/Community Connections**. Students can work in pairs or small groups to prepare their projects.

Presentation and Explanation

❏ *Lesson Opener:* Have students look at the pictures on pages 88–89 and read *Accent sur....* Ask them to point out which of these activities they enjoy doing. Help them read the captions for the photos. Explain the PHOTO CULTURE NOTES on page T89.

❏ *Vocabulary A:* To introduce talking about preferences, play **Audio** 13.1 or **Video** 13.1–2, or model the expressions in *Préférences*, pages 90–91, using **Overhead Visuals** Transparencies 14a and b to clarify meanings. Point out the *Préférences* box on pages 90–91. Have students talk about their own likes and dislikes using the expressions.

❏ *Vocabulary B:* Present *Souhaits*, page 93. After modeling the expressions, have students repeat. Point out the verb forms in the box. Ask students to complete the expressions with their own wishes.

❏ *Vocabulary C:* As you model *Invitations*, page 94, use gestures and intonation to help clarify meanings of expressions for accepting and turning down an invitation. Play **Video** 13.3 or **Audio** 13.3–4. Have students repeat the questions and expressions.

❏ Introduce information about the French telephone system by playing **Video** 13.5 or reading that section in the **Video Script**, page 26. Students can comment on similarities and differences in public telephones in France and in the U.S.

Guided Practice and Checking Understanding

❏ Have students practice expressing preferences, wishes, and invitations with **Overhead Visuals** Transparencies S9 and 14a and b, using the activities on pages A18 and A64–A65.

❏ To check listening comprehension, use the **Audio** or read from the **Cassette Script** as students do **Activity Book** activities B–F on pages 89–92.

❏ Play the **Video** or read from the **Video Script** and have students do **Video Activity Book** activities 1–6, pages 49–52.

❏ Use the TPR activity on page T90 for practice talking about everyday activities.

Independent Practice

❑ Model the activities on pages 90–94. For activity 1, follow the suggestions in ORAL INTRODUCTION, page T90, and COOPERATIVE GROUP PRACTICE, page T91. Activities 2, 5, 6, and 7 can be completed for homework. Activities 3, 4, 8, and 9 can be done in pairs. Have students check their answers with the **Answer Key**.

❑ Have pairs of students do **Communipak** Interview 3, Tu as la parole 1–3, Échange 1, or Tête à tête 1 (pages 56–64), or **Video Activity Book** Activité 7, page 52.

Monitoring and Adjusting

❑ Have students complete the Writing Activities on **Activity Book** pages 105–106.

❑ As students work on the activities on pages 90–94, monitor language used for preferences, wishes, and invitations. Refer them back to the boxes on pages 90–91, 93, and 94 as needed. The suggestions for the VARIATION and CHALLENGE activities on pages T92–T94 can be used to meet all students' needs.

❑ Do **Teaching to Multiple Intelligences** activities 1 and 2 on pages 57–59 to monitor students' understanding of vocabulary and use of language for expressing wishes.

❑ Use the **Writing Template** to monitor production of the lesson's content.

Assessment

❑ Administer Quiz 13 on pages 55–56 of **Lesson Quizzes** after completing the lesson's activities. Adjust lesson quizzes to the class's specific needs by using the **Test Bank**.

Reteaching

❑ Redo any appropriate activities from the **Activity Book**.

❑ Students can use the **CD-ROM** or **Video** to review portions of the lesson.

Extension and Enrichment

❑ Individual students can use the **CD-ROM** for extension and enrichment.

❑ If students are interested, have them do **Internet Connection Notes** Internet Project 1 or 2 on pages 27–30 to explore Internet sites for recreational activities.

Summary and Closure

❑ Have students prepare the role plays described in the Goal 1 activity on page A18 of **Overhead Visuals**, using Transparency S9. As they present their role plays, ask others to summarize the communicative functions that they have heard in this lesson.

❑ You may wish to have students prepare activity 5 on page 95 for inclusion in their Written Portfolios.

End-of-Lesson Activities

❑ À votre tour!: Arrange students in pairs to practice activities 1 and 2 on page 95. Assign any or all of activities 3–5 for homework. Follow the suggestions in the TE margin for COOPERATIVE READING PRACTICE.

UNITÉ 4, LEÇON 14: *Qui est là?*, PAGE 96

Objectives

Communicative Functions and Topics	To talk about where people are
	To ask and answer yes/no questions
	To express negation
Linguistic Goals	To use subject pronouns
	To use the verb *être* and the negative *ne... pas*
	To use yes/no questions with *est-ce que*
	To pronounce the vowel /a/
Cultural Goals	To talk about where French young people spend their free time

Motivation and Focus

❑   Have students look at the photos on page 97. Ask where the students in the photos are and what they are doing. Talk about places students like to go after school or on weekends. You might play the **Video** for Module 14 as an introduction to the lesson.

Presentation and Explanation

❑   *Lesson Opener:* Use the SETTING THE STAGE activity, page T96. Check understanding with the *Compréhension* activity on page 96. Have students read the conversation and discuss what they think it is about.

❑   *Note culturelle:* Read *Le mercredi après-midi*, page 97. Do the CROSS-CULTURAL OBSERVATION on page T97 after students view **Video** 14.4, Au café, or after you read that section in the **Video Script**, page 28.

❑   *Grammar A:* Use **Overhead Visuals** Transparency 16 to present and explain subject pronouns and the verb *être*, as presented in the grammar box on page 98. Point out forms students have already practiced. See the notes in the TE margin. Introduce questions with *où* using **Overhead Visuals** Transparency 15. Point out location expressions in the vocabulary box, page 99.

❑   *Grammar B:* Present yes/no questions with *est-ce que* and expressions to answer them, pages 100–101. Give statements; have students respond with a yes/no question.

❑   *Grammar C:* Present negatives and useful words, pages 102–103. Practice using these forms with SPEAKING PRACTICE, page T102, and **Overhead Visuals** Transparency 15.

❑   *Prononciation:* Have students read the box on page 103. Play **Audio** 14.6, or model the words and have students repeat.

Guided Practice and Checking Understanding

❑   Practice affirmative and negative verb forms and where and yes/no questions with **Overhead Visuals** Transparencies 14a and b and 15.

❑   Play the **Audio** or read the **Cassette Script** and have students do **Activity Book** activities C–F on pages 93–95.

❑   Have students complete **Video Activity Book** activities 1–4, pages 53–56, as they watch the **Video** or listen to you read the **Video Script**.

❑   Check understanding of places and questions with *où* using the TPR activity, page T99.

Independent Practice

❑   Do activities 1–10, pages 99–103. Students can work alone or for homework on 1, 2, 5, 7, 9, and 10. Do 3, 4, 6, and 8 on text pages 100–102 as COOPERATIVE PAIR PRACTICE. Have students check their answers with the **Answer Key**.

❑   Use **Communipak** Tête à tête 1, pages 63–64, or **Video Activity Book** activity 5, page 56, for pair or group practice.

Monitoring and Adjusting

❑ Monitor students' writing as they work with **Activity Book** Writing Activities 1–5 on pages 107–108.

❑ Point out and discuss the grammar explanations on pages 98–103. Help with pronunciation and tag questions using the TEACHING NOTES on pages T100 and T101.

❑ Use activities 3 and 4 on pages 60–62 of **Teaching to Multiple Intelligences** to monitor students' use of *où* and the verb *être* in its different forms.

❑ Monitor students' written production with the **Writing Template**.

Assessment

❑ After students have completed the lesson's activities, administer Quiz 14 on pages 57–58 of **Lesson Quizzes**. Use the **Test Bank** to adapt questions to your class's needs.

Reteaching

❑ If students have difficulty with any of the activities in the **Activity Book**, reteach the content and have them redo the activity.

❑ Individual students can use the **CD-ROM** or **Video** to review portions of the lesson.

❑ Use **Teacher to Teacher**, pages 7 and 8, to reteach *être*.

Extension and Enrichment

❑ Individual students can use the **CD-ROM** for extension and enrichment.

❑ Play the LISTENING GAME on page T103.

❑ Students can choose Internet Project 3 or 4 on pages 31–32 of **Internet Connection Notes** for exploring French chat rooms or using a French version of Carmen Sandiego.

Summary and Closure

❑ Have pairs of students present role plays as described in the activity at the top of **Overhead Visuals** page A65. Other students can summarize linguistic and communicative goals demonstrated in the role plays.

❑ Do PORTFOLIO ASSESSMENT as suggested on page T105.

End-of-Lesson Activities

❑ *À votre tour!:* Do the activities on pages 104–105. Students can work individually on activities 1–2 and 4–5. Have students work in small groups to practice and present to the class the *Créa-dialogue* activity on page 105.

UNITÉ 4, LEÇON 15: *Une boum,* PAGE 106

Objectives

Communicative Functions and Topics   To describe what one person or several people are doing or are not doing

To talk about what people like and don't like to do

To express approval or regret

Linguistic Goals   To use verb + infinitive

To use regular *-er* verbs

To pronounce vowels /i/ and /u/

Cultural Goals   To become familiar with French party customs

Motivation and Focus

❑   Have students look at the pictures on page 107 and discuss what is happening. Discuss party organization with SETTING THE STAGE on page T106. You may show the **Video** to preview the lesson. Have students comment on the activities mentioned.

Presentation and Explanation

❑   *Lesson Opener:* Read the introductory paragraph on page 106 and invite students to guess what Jean-Marc is going to say to Béatrice. Play **Video** 15.4 or **Audio** 15.1, the opening conversation. Ask students to read and summarize the conversation. Share the information in the PHOTO CULTURE NOTE in the TE margin.

❑   *Note culturelle:* Have students read *Une boum,* page 107. Encourage them to compare French and American parties by playing the **Video** or reading the **Video Script** for 15.5. Explain the PHOTO CULTURE NOTES on page T107.

❑   *Grammar A, B,* and *C:* Present *-er* verbs with **Overhead Visuals** Transparencies 14a and b and 17. Explain verb conjugations, pointing out the grammar boxes and information on pages 108 and 110. Practice verb endings using Transparency 16. Introduce affirmative and negative forms on page 112.

❑   *Vocabulaire:* Model and explain the words and expressions in the boxes on page 114. Point out examples of verb + infinitive that students have already practiced. Have students read the grammar explanation on page 115.

❑   *Prononciation:* Model pronunciation of the vowels /i/ and /u/, page 115, and have students repeat the words. Practice pronunciation with **Audio** 15.6.

Guided Practice and Checking Understanding

❑   Use **Overhead Visuals** Transparency 17 and the suggestions on page A68 for practice with *-er* verbs. To practice expressions for how often and how well, have students ask and answer questions about the pictures on Transparencies 14a and b.

❑   Check listening skills with the **Audio** or the **Cassette Script** and **Activity Book** activities C–F, pages 97–99.

❑   Have students do **Video Activity Book** pages 57–59 as they view the **Video** or listen while you read the **Video Script**.

❑   Use the TPR activities on pages T109 and T110 to check students' understanding of verbs and subject pronouns.

Independent Practice

❑   Practice with the activities on pages 108–115. Assign activities 3, 5, 7, and 9–12 for homework. Use any or all of activities 1, 2, 4, 6, 8, 13, or 14 for COOPERATIVE PAIR PRACTICE. Have students check their answers with the **Answer Key**. Follow the suggestions for COOPERATIVE WRITING PRACTICE, page T111, for activity 8.

❑ Have pairs of students choose one of the following **Communipak** activities: Interviews 1, 2; Tu as la parole 4, 5, 6; Conversations 1, 2; Échange 2; Tête à tête 1 (pages 55–64). They may also do page 60 of the **Video Activity Book**.

Monitoring and Adjusting

❑ Have students do the Writing Activities on **Activity Book** pages 109–112.
❑ Monitor students' work on the activities on pages 108–117. Have them review the grammar and vocabulary boxes as needed. Use the TEACHING TIPS and TEACHING NOTE, and explain the PRONUNCIATION and LANGUAGE NOTES, on pages T108–T114.
❑ Use **Teaching to Multiple Intelligences** activities 5, 6, and 7, pages 63–69.
❑ Use the **Writing Template** to monitor students' written production.

Assessment

❑ Administer Quiz 15 on pages 59–60 of **Lesson Quizzes** after completing the lesson. Use the **Test Bank** to adapt the quiz questions to your class's needs.

Reteaching

❑ Redo any appropriate activities from the **Activity book**.
❑ Use the **CD-ROM** or **Video** to reteach portions of the lesson.
❑ Follow the suggestions for VARIATIONS of activities 4 and 6, pages T110–T111. **Teacher to Teacher**, page 9, can also be used for additional practice of verb forms.

Extension and Enrichment

❑ Individual students can use the **CD-ROM** for extension and enrichment.
❑ Play the GAME described on page T113. Students can also do the CHALLENGE activity on page T117 to prepare their own illustrated messages.
❑ Students can explore international holidays or communicate with penpals with **Internet Connection Notes** projects 5 and 6, pages 33–34.

Summary and Closure

❑ Use **Overhead Visuals** Transparency S10, with the Goal 1 activity on page A19 and the Goal 1 activity on page A20, to have students summarize the communicative and cultural goals of the lesson.
❑ Do PORTFOLIO ASSESSMENT on page T117.

End-of-Lesson Activities

❑ *À votre tour!:* Have students work in small groups to do activities 1, 2, 3, and 4 on pages 116–117. They can check answers with the **Answer Key** or **Audio**. Have students write their personal responses to activity 5 and share them with the class.

UNITÉ 4, LEÇON 16: *Une interview*, PAGE 118

Objectives

Communicative Functions and Topics
To ask for information and to ask about people
To ask and to describe what people are doing
To express mild doubt or surprise

Linguistic Goals
To use the verb *faire*
To ask information questions with *est-ce que* and to form questions with inversion
To pronounce the vowel /y/

Cultural Goals
To be aware of French heritage in Senegal
To learn about UNESCO headquarters in Paris

Motivation and Focus

❏ Ask students to preview the photos on pages 118–119. Ask where they think these pictures were taken. Then do SETTING THE SCENE, page T118. You may then use the **Video** to present the lesson. Have students comment on the scenes and conversations.

Presentation and Explanation

❏ *Lesson Opener:* Read the introductory paragraph on page 118. Ask students to suggest interview questions. Play **Video** 16.4 or **Audio** 16.1, or model the opening conversation. Have students read and summarize the dialogue.

❏ *Notes culturelles:* Read *Le Sénégal* and *L'UNESCO* on pages 118–119. Show **Video** 16.5 or read the **Video Script**. Do the CROSS-CULTURAL OBSERVATION, page T118.

❏ *Grammar A* and *Vocabulaire:* Review times and activities with the WARM-UP AND REVIEW activity, page T120. Present information questions on page 120, pointing out intonation patterns. Introduce interrogative words in the *Vocabularire* box, page 120.

❏ *Grammar B* and *C:* Present expressions with *qui*, page 122, and *qu'est-ce que?*, page 123. Use the question words to ask about students' activities.

❏ *Grammar D* and *Vocabulaire:* Present *faire* and expressions with *faire*, page 124. Practice by making sentences with *faire* using **Overhead Visuals** Transparency 18.

❏ *Grammar E:* Introduce inversion, page 125, as another way to ask questions in French. Point out word order in affirmative and interrogative forms.

❏ *Prononciation:* Model or use **Audio** 16.6 to present and practice pronunciation of the vowel /y/. Students can read the information in the *Prononciation* box, page 125.

Guided Practice and Checking Understanding

❏ Use **Overhead Visuals** Transparency 18 and the activities described on page A70 to have students practice expressions with *faire*.

❏ To check understanding, use **Audio** or the **Cassette Script** with **Activity Book** activities C–F, pages 102–103.

❏ Play the **Video** or read the **Video Script** and have students do **Video Activity Book** pages 61–63.

Independent Practice

❏ Model the activities on pages 121–125. Students can do 4 and 9–11 alone or for homework and 1–3 and 5–8 for COOPERATIVE PAIR PRACTICE, checking their work with the **Answer Key**.

❏ The **Video Activity Book**, page 64, and **Communipak** Interview 4, page 56, Conversations 1–4, pages 59–60, Échange 2, page 62, and Tête à tête 3, pages 67–68, can be used for additional oral pair practice.

Monitoring and Adjusting

❏ Assign Writing Activities 1–5 in the **Activity Book**, pages 113–115.
❏ Monitor students as they work on the practice activities. Refer them to appropriate grammar and vocabulary boxes, pages 120–125. Use Language and Pronunciation notes and Teaching strategies, pages T121–T125.
❏ Use **Teaching to Multiple Intelligences** activities 8–11 on pages 70–77 to monitor students' understanding of verb forms and question formation.

Assessment

❏ After students have completed all of the lesson's activities, administer Quiz 16 on pages 61–62 of **Lesson Quizzes**. Use the **Test Bank** to adapt questions to your class's needs. Administer Unit Test 4 (Form A or B) on pages 43–51 of **Unit Tests**. For additional assessment of specific language skills, use the **Proficiency Tests** for the unit. You may also administer Comprehensive Test 1(Form A or B) on pages C-3–C-26 of **Comprehensive (Semester) Tests**.

Reteaching

❏ Redo any appropriate activities from the **Activity Book**.
❏ Assign the **CD-ROM** or **Video** for students who need more review or make-up work.

Extension and Enrichment

❏ Individual students can use the **CD-ROM** for extension and enrichment.
❏ Play the Game: Getting acquainted, page T122.
❏ Students can learn more about Senegal, UNESCO, or French TV with the **Internet Connection Notes** activities 7–9, pages 35–37.

Summary and Closure

❏ Have pairs of students prepare role play interviews modeled on the opening conversation on pages 118–119. As they present the interviews, have other students summarize the linguistic and communicative goals of the lesson.
❏ Do Portfolio assessment on page T127.

End-of-Unit Activities

❏ *À votre tour!:* Do the activities on pages 126–127. Students can check their own work on 1 and 3 with the **Audio** or **Cassette Script**. Have pairs prepare and present the role plays in activities 2 and 4. Students can practice writing questions in activities 5 and 6.
❏ *Entracte 4:* Follow the suggestions in the TE margins to read the selections on pages 128–133. Encourage reading for meaning using cognates and context clues. Discuss the *Notes culturelles*, pages 130 and 132. Do the letter-writing activity, page 131.
❏ *Reading and Culture Activities:* Use **Activity Book** pages 117–120 to review cultural information and activities.

UNITÉ 5, LEÇON 17: *Les personnes et les objets*, PAGE 136

Objectives

Communicative Functions and Topics
To describe people's physical appearance and age

To identify objects

To discuss what one owns and doesn't own, and whether these things work or not

To describe one's room, what's in it, and where things are located

Linguistic Goals To use the expression *il y a*

Cultural Goals To learn about the multi-cultural reality of contemporary France

Motivation and Focus

❏ Ask students to describe the people and activities in the photos of the *Unit Opener*, pages 134–135. Share the PHOTO CULTURE NOTES, page T135. Students can point out any common interests they have with the students in the photos.

❏ Read *Accent sur...*, page 136. Guide students to note common attitudes, beliefs, and interests of French young people. Have students read the captions for the photos on page 137, explaining the PHOTO CULTURE NOTES in the TE margin. Help them make comparisons to the U.S. by sharing the facts about the U.S. in CULTURAL NOTES in the TE margin. Do MULTI-CULTURALISM IN FRANCE on page T137.

❏ Introduce the project on pages 58–60 of **Interdisciplinary/Community Connections**. Divide students into groups and help them plan their projects.

Presentation and Explanation

❏ *Vocabulary A:* Introduce the vocabulary and expressions for describing people on pages 138–139 with **Overhead Visuals** Transparency 19. Model or play **Audio** 17.1. Point out masculine and feminine forms of adjectives.

❏ *Vocabulary B:* Use **Overhead Visuals** Transparency 20 to present the names of objects on page 140. As you introduce nouns, remind students to note if nouns are masculine or feminine. Model expressions and object names for students to repeat.

❏ *Vocabulary C:* Present the names of personal possessions on page 142 with **Overhead Visuals** Transparency 21. Have students identify which possessions they have.

❏ *Vocabulary D:* Use **Overhead Visuals** Transparencies 22 and 23 to introduce furnishings, parts of a room, and prepositions, page 144. Help students use *il y a* to talk about what is in a place.

Guided Practice and Checking Understanding

❏ Use **Overhead Visuals** Transparencies 19–23, with the activities described on pages A72 and A74–A78, to practice the expressions introduced in this lesson.

❏ Have students listen to the **Audio** or **Cassette Script** as they do **Activity Book** activities A–F on pages 125–128.

❏ Students can do **Video Activity Book** activities 1–6 on pages 65–68 as they watch the **Video** or listen to the **Video Script**.

❏ Check understanding of the vocabulary and expressions presented by using TPR: DESCRIPTIVE ADJECTIVES, page T138, and TPR: EVERYDAY OBJECTS, page T140.

Independent Practice

❏ Model the activities on pages 139–146 and then have students do them alone or for homework. Follow the suggestions for COOPERATIVE PAIR PRACTICE with activities 3–4, 7–8, 11, and 13. Have them check their work using the **Answer Key**.

❏ Use **Communipak** Tu as la parole 5–7, Conversations 1–2, Échange 1, and Tête à tête 1–2 (pages 76–86) for additional pair practice. Play the group game in **Video Activity Book** activity 7, page 68.

Monitoring and Adjusting

❏ Assign Writing Activities 1–7 on pages 141–144 of the **Activity Book**.

❏ Monitor students as they work on practice activities. Have students study the vocabulary boxes on pages 138–144 as needed. Use the suggestions for VARIATION, page T141, and EXPANSION, pages T143 and T145, to challenge more advanced students. Do SPEAKING PRACTICE, page T142, to help describe objects.

❏ Do **Teaching to Multiple Intelligences** activities 1–4 on pages 78–85 to monitor students' use of descriptive adjectives, object names, and prepositions of location.

Assessment

❏ Administer Quiz 17 on pages 63–64 of **Lesson Quizzes** after completing the lesson. The **Test Bank** can be used to adjust the lesson quiz to students' needs.

Reteaching

❏ Use **Teacher to Teacher**, page 10, for reteaching.

❏ Assign portions of the **CD-ROM** or **Video** to reteach parts of the lesson.

Extension and Enrichment

❏ If students are interested, have them choose one of the **Internet Connection Notes** projects on pages 41–44 to learn more about people and their possessions.

❏ Introduce the SUPPLEMENTARY VOCABULARY on page T139, and have students practice using these words to describe people they know or pictures of people. You may also play the GAME: QUI EST-CE?, page T139.

Summary and Closure

❏ Use **Overhead Visuals** Transparency S12 and the activity on page A24 to have students demonstrate describing people. Include a summary of object vocabulary by asking them to tell what the people on the transparency want for their birthdays. Ask other students to summarize the lesson goals.

❏ Do PORTFOLIO ASSESSMENT on page T147.

End-of-Lesson Activities

❏ *À votre tour!:* Do activities 1 and 2, page 147. Follow the suggestions for COOPERATIVE PRACTICE, having students check their conversations in the **Answer Key**. Assign written self-expression activities 3 and 4 for homework.

UNITÉ 5, LEÇON 18: *Vive la différence!*, PAGE 148

Objectives

Communicative Functions and Topics
- To talk about what one has
- To identify and designate people and things
- To express negation
- To make generalizations
- To discuss repeated events
- To contradict a negative statement or question

Linguistic Goals
- To use singular/plural and masculine/feminine nouns
- To use the verb *avoir* and expressions with *avoir*
- To use definite articles in general statements and to indicate repeated events
- To use the indefinite article and the negative article *pas de*
- To pronounce the articles *le* and *les*

Cultural Goals
- To learn about Montpellier and Strasbourg

Motivation and Focus

❏ Have students describe the two friends' pictures on page 148. Ask them to suggest similarities and differences between the two friends. Have students talk about what common interests they have with friends and what things make them individuals.

Presentation and Explanation

❏ *Lesson Opener:* Play **Audio** 18.1, or read page 148, with students' books closed. Ask students to read the page and discuss similarities and differences between the two friends.

❏ *Note culturelle:* Read and discuss *Montpellier et Strasbourg*, page 149. Guide discussion of how these two French cities are different from each other. Explain the PHOTO CULTURE NOTES on page T149.

❏ *Grammar A and Vocabulaire:* Introduce the verb *avoir* and expressions with *avoir*, page 150. Have students ask and answer questions about things they have.

❏ *Grammar B:* Present masculine and feminine nouns, articles, and pronouns, page 151. Remind students of the definite and indefinite articles they studied in previous lessons.

❏ *Grammar C:* Introduce plural nouns and articles, pages 152–153. Point out the regular plural ending *-s* (silent in spoken French) and the plural articles *les* and *des*.

❏ *Grammar D:* Present use of the indefinite article in negative statements, page 154. Introduce the use of *si* to contradict a negative statement or question, page 155.

❏ *Grammar E and F:* Present the use of definite articles in making generalizations, page 156, and in talking about habitual events with days of the week, page 157. Use the LANGUAGE NOTES in the TE margins to point out contrasts with English.

❏ *Prononciation:* Use **Audio** 18.6 to model pronunciation of the articles *le* and *les*. Have students practice repeating the words in the box, page 157.

Guided Practice and Checking Understanding

❏ Use **Overhead Visuals** Transparencies 24 and 25, with the activities on pages A79–A81, to practice expressing negation and using articles with days of the week.

❏ Check understanding of the opening text, vocabulary, and expressions with **Activity Book** activities C–F, pages 129–131, and **Audio** 18.2–18.5, or the **Cassette Script**.

❏ Have students watch the **Video**, or listen to the **Video Script**, while they complete **Video Activity Book** ages 69–71.

❏ Use the TPR activity, page T152, to reteach singular and plural forms.

Independent Practice

❏ Model the activities on pages 150–157. Students can work alone on 1, 2, 6, 8, 10, and 12–16, or do them for homework. Model exchanges and arrange students in pairs to practice activities 3–5, 7, 9, and 11. They may check their work with the **Answer Key**.

❏ Use **Communipak** Interviews 3–4 and Tu as la parole 1–4 (pages 74–75) for pair practice. Students can do the pair guessing game on **Video Activity Book** page 72.

Monitoring and Adjusting

❏ Assign the Writing Activities on pages 145–148 of the **Activity Book**.

❏ Use TEACHING and LANGUAGE notes, pages T150–T157, to explain vocabulary and reinforce grammar. Check singular/plural nouns with the LISTENING ACTIVITY on page T153. Use the TEACHING STRATEGY on page T154 to monitor use of *il y a*.

❏ Use **Teaching to Multiple Intelligences** activity 5, pages 86–88, to practice the use of *avoir*, *pas* + *un*, *des*, *pas de*, and *si*.

Assessment

❏ After students have completed all of the lesson's activities, administer Quiz 18 on pages 65–66 of **Lesson Quizzes**. Use the **Test Bank** to adapt questions to your needs.

Reteaching

❏ Redo any activities in the **Activity Book** that caused students difficulty.

❏ Students can use the **CD-ROM** or **Video** to review the lesson.

Extension and Enrichment

❏ Individual students can use the **CD-ROM** for extension and enrichment.

❏ Introduce the past tense, using the material on pages T150–T151 and T157.

❏ Assign one of the projects in **Internet Connection Notes** project 4, pages 45–46.

Summary and Closure

❏ Invite pairs of students to present any of the **Communipak** or oral *À votre tour!* activities to the class. Help other students recall and summarize the vocabulary and grammar they have learned in the lesson.

❏ Do PORTFOLIO ASSESSMENT on page T159.

End-of-Lesson Activities

❏ *À votre tour!:* Do any or all of the activities on pages 158–159. Students can work individually on activities 1 and 4–6 and in pairs to practice and present the *Créa-dialogue* activity 3 on page 159. Assign the survey in activity 2 as an extra project.

UNITÉ 5, LEÇON 19: *Le copain de Mireille,* PAGE 160

Objectives

Communicative Functions and Topics
To describe people and objects
To talk about character traits and nationality
To talk about where things are made
To introduce a conclusion

Linguistic Goals
To understand adjective formation and position
To pronounce final consonants on feminine forms but not on masculine forms

Cultural Goals
To understand the importance of friendship for the French

Motivation and Focus

❑ Look at the photos on pages 160–161. Where are these people? What are they doing and talking about? Conduct a brief discussion on friendship. Have the class complete the sentence "*Un copain (une copine) est* ...."

Presentation and Explanation

❑ *Lesson Opener:* Use the suggestions for SETTING THE SCENE, page T160. Play **Video** 19.4 or **Audio** 19.1, or model the conversation on page 160. Ask students to read and summarize the conversation.

❑ *Note culturelle:* Read and discuss *L'amitié,* page 161. Explain the PHOTO CULTURE NOTE in the TE margin. Encourage students to compare French and American concepts of how important friends are, and what qualities are desirable in friends.

❑ *Grammar A, Vocabulaire,* and *Grammar B:* Use **Overhead Visuals** Transparency 26a and the overlay (b) to present descriptive adjectives. Explain masculine and feminine forms, page 162, and point them out in the *Vocabularire* box on page 163. Play **Audio** 19.3 to model pronunciation of the adjective forms. Introduce plural adjectives on page 164; explain the LANGUAGE NOTE in the TE margin.

❑ *Vocabulaire* and *Grammar C:* Review adjectives of nationality and introduce new ones with **Overhead Visuals** Transparency 27. Point out masculine, feminine, and plural forms of the nationality adjectives, page 165. Remind students that nationalities are not capitalized in French. Introduce and practice **alors** to introduce a conclusion. Explain placement of adjectives, page 166.

❑ *Prononciation:* Guide students to distinguish between masculine and feminine forms of adjectives by noting final consonant pronunciation, page 167. Model or use **Audio** 19.6 and have students repeat.

Guided Practice and Checking Understanding

❑ Use **Overhead Visuals** Transparencies 26 and 27, with the activities on pages A82–A83 and A85, to practice describing people.

❑ Use **Audio** 19.2–5, or the **Cassette Script**, with **Activity Book** activities C–F, pages 133–135.

❑ Play the **Video** or read the **Video Script** while students do **Video Activity Book** pages 73–77.

❑ Practice masculine and feminine adjectives with the TPR activity, page T162.

Independent Practice

❑ Assign the activities on pages 162–167. Students can prepare and practice 1–5 and 7–10 for homework. Have students check their responses with the **Answer Key**. Model and have students repeat the exchanges in activity 6, having them practice in pairs.

❑ Choose any or all of the following pair/group practice activities: **Communipak** Conversations 3–4 on pages 77–78, Échange 2 on page 82, or Tête à tête 3 on pages 87–88. In small groups, have students do **Video Activity Book** page 78.

Monitoring and Adjusting

❑ Assign Writing Activities 1–7 on pages 149–152 of the **Activity Book**.

❑ Monitor students' use of adjectives as they work on the practice activities. Point out and explain the grammar and vocabulary boxes as needed. Explain the LANGUAGE NOTES on pages T162–T165.

❑ Monitor students' pronunciation of final consonants as they participate in oral activities. Use activities 6 and 7 on pages 89–93 in **Teaching to Multiple Intelligences** to monitor understanding of descriptive adjectives and to adjust pronunciation.

Assessment

❑ Administer Quiz 19 on pages 67–68 of **Lesson Quizzes** after the lesson's activities are completed. Use the **Test Bank** to adapt the quiz to your class's particular needs.

Reteaching

❑ If students have difficulty with any of the activities in the **Activity Book**, redo them.

❑ Students can use the **CD-ROM** or **Video** to review parts of the lesson as needed.

Extension and Enrichment

❑ To extend the practice of describing people, introduce SUPPLEMENTARY VOCABULARY and play the GAME: DESCRIPTIONS, page T163. Introduce more nationalities, page T165.

❑ For students who are ready to use the past tense, do TALKING ABOUT PAST EVENTS, pages T164–T165.

❑ Students can explore and describe favorite websites with **Internet Connection Notes** projects 5 and 6, pages 47–48.

Summary and Closure

❑ Collect the letters students wrote in **Activity Book** activity 7 on page 152. Read them aloud, omitting the name of the writer. Have others guess who wrote the letter. Point out descriptive adjectives used.

❑ Do PORTFOLIO ASSESSMENT on page T169.

End-of-Lesson Activities

❑ *À votre tour!:* Use activities 1–3, pages 167–169, for COOPERATIVE PAIR PRACTICE. Explain the CULTURAL BACKGROUND information on page T169. Have students choose any one of activities 4–6 to prepare as a written homework assignment.

UNITÉ 5, LEÇON 20: *La voiture de Roger*, PAGE 170

Objectives

Communicative Functions and Topics
To use adjectives of aspect and color to describe possessions

To get someone's attention

To express opinions

Linguistic Goals
To use *il est* and *c'est*

To position adjectives correctly

To pronounce the letters "*ch*"

Cultural Goals
To learn about French people and their automobiles

Motivation and Focus

❏   As students preview the photos on pages 170–171, invite comments on cars and driving. Discuss the cars and auto company pictured. Encourage students to share other information they know about the French auto industry.

Presentation and Explanation

❏   *Lesson Opener:* Present the opening dialogue on page 170 with **Video** 20.4, **Audio** 20.1, or by acting it out. Have students read the dialogue and guess what it is about. Explain the PHOTO CULTURE NOTE, page T170.

❏   *Note culturelle:* Read and discuss *Les Français et l'auto,* page 171. Explain the PHOTO CULTURE NOTE, page T171. Show **Video** 20.5 or play **Audio** 20.6. Have students guess the meanings of words in the photo on page 171.

❏   *Grammar A* and *Vocabulaire:* Introduce colors, page 172, with **Overhead Visuals** Transparency 28. Point out form and position. Practice with objects in the classroom.

❏   *Grammar B* and *Vocabulaire:* Introduce and practice adjective placement, page 173. Point out that the adjectives in the box are placed before the nouns.

❏   *Vocabulary:* Present and practice getting someone's attention with the expressions in the vocabulary box on page 174.

❏   *Grammar C* and *D* and *Vocabulaire:* Present use of *il est* and *c'est* for describing people and things, page 175. Introduce expressing opinions, page 176. Point out use of *c'est* and useful vocabulary and expressions.

❏   *Prononciation:* Play or model **Audio** 20.7 and have students practice pronunciation of *ch*, page 177. Use the PRONUNCIATION NOTES in the TE margin.

Guided Practice and Checking Understanding

❏   Use **Overhead Visuals** Transparencies 28 and 29, with the activities on page A87, to practice colors and adjectives that precede the noun.

❏   Use **Audio** 20.2–6, or the **Cassette Script**, with **Activity Book** activities D–G, pages 137–139.

❏   Use the **Video** or **Video Script** for pages 79–81 in the **Video Activity Book**.

❏   To practice colors and adjective placement, use the TPR activity on colors, page T172.

Independent Practice

❏   Do the activities on pages 172–177. Have students do 3–4 alone or for homework. Model 1, 2, 5, 7, and 8 and do them as COOPERATIVE PAIR PRACTICE. Assign 6 for homework. Have students use the **Answer Key** to check their work.

❏ Use **Communipak** Tu as la parole 8 (page 76) or Conversations 5 and 6 (pages 79–80) or **Video Activity Book**, page 82, for additional pair and group practice.

Monitoring and Adjusting

❏ **Activity Book** Writing Activities 1–7, pages 153–156, can be assigned for homework.

❏ Monitor students as they work on practice activities. Point out grammar and vocabulary boxes, pages 172–176. Follow the suggestions for the TEACHING STRATEGY on page T172 and the SPEAKING ACTIVITY on page T175.

❏ Have students work with **Teaching to Multiple Intelligences** activity 8, pages 94–95, for extra practice with adjective placement.

Assessment

❏ Use Quiz 20 on pages 69–70 of **Lesson Quizzes** after completing the lesson. Give Unit Test 5 (Form A or B) on pages 52–60 of **Unit Tests**. Select appropriate **Proficiency Tests** for the unit. Any of the test questions can be modified using the **Test Bank**.

Reteaching

❏ Redo any of the activities in the **Activity Book** that cause students difficulty.

❏ Review **c'est** and **il est** with USING CHANTS and the SPEAKING ACTIVITY on pages T174–T175. Do the puzzle on page 11 of **Teacher to Teacher**.

❏ Assign the **CD-ROM** or **Video** for review and reteaching.

Extension and Enrichment

❏ Individual students may use the **CD-ROM** for extension and enrichment.

❏ Use **Internet Connection Notes** projects 7, 8, and 9, pages 49–51, to learn more about European cars, mopeds, Toulouse, and aviation in France.

Summary and Closure

❏ Guide students to summarize what they have learned in this lesson. Then encourage them to use what they have learned as they describe the people and things on **Overhead Visuals** Transparency S11.

❏ Do PORTFOLIO ASSESSMENT on page T179.

End-of-Unit Activities

❏ *À votre tour!:* Choose any or all activities on pages 178–179. Use the **Audio** to check responses in activities 1 and 2. Arrange students in pairs to role play activity 3. Have students practice composition with activities 4 or 5.

❏ *Entracte 5:* Follow the PRE-READING and POST-READING suggestions and notes in the TE margins, pages 180–185. Help students use cognates and context clues to aid in comprehension as they read.

❏ *Reading and Culture Activities:* Have students do **Activity Book** pages 157–160.

UNITÉ 6, LEÇON 21: *La ville et la maison*, PAGE 188

Objectives

Communicative Functions and Topics
To identify and describe city places, streets, buildings, and neighborhoods
To ask for and give directions
To give your address
To describe the inside and outside of your home

Linguistic Goals To use impersonal *il y a* and *c'est*

Cultural Goals To learn about two French cities: Paris and Tours

Motivation and Focus

❏ Have students look at the photos in the *Unit Opener*, pages 186–187. Share the information in the PHOTO CULTURE NOTES, page T187. Discuss similarities and differences between Paris and their city or town. Read *Thème et Objectifs*, page 187.

❏ Do SETTING THE SCENE, page T188. Then read together *Accent sur...*, page 188, and the descriptions of city places on page 189. Share the CULTURAL NOTE and the PHOTO CULTURE NOTE in the TE margins.

❏ Introduce the project on pages 61–63 of **Interdisciplinary/Community Connections**. Divide the class into groups and help them begin to plan their projects.

Presentation and Explanation

❏ *Vocabulary A:* Present page 190, modeling and having students repeat. Help students describe their city or town and give their own addresses in French.

❏ *Note culturelle:* Read *Le nom des rues*, page 190. Discuss streets in your city or town that are named after famous people.

❏ *Vocabulary B:* Use **Overhead Visuals** Transparencies 30a and b to introduce place names, page 191. Have students identify places that are located in their city or town.

❏ *Vocabulary C:* Introduce page 193, asking and giving directions. As you model the sentences, help clarify meaning with gestures and intonation.

❏ *Vocabulary D:* To present rooms of the house, page 194, use **Overhead Visuals** Transparency 31. Share the CULTURAL and LANGUAGE NOTES on page T194. Model and have students repeat the expressions; guide them to describe their own homes.

Guided Practice and Checking Understanding

❏ Use **Overhead Visuals** Transparencies 30a and b, 31, and 32, with the activities on pages A88–A94, to practice talking about cities and houses and giving directions.

❏ Check students' listening skills with **Audio** 21.1–8 or the **Cassette Script**, and **Activity Book** activities A–F on pages 165–168.

❏ Have students do **Video Activity Book** pages 83–87 as they watch the **Video** or listen to the **Video Script** for the lesson.

❏ Do the TPR activities on places, page T190, and on rooms of the house, pages T194–T195.

Independent Practice

❏ Do the practice activities on pages 190–195. Do 1, 3, and 6–8 for homework. Model activities 2, 4, and 5 before having students do them as COOPERATIVE PAIR PRACTICE. Have students check their work with the **Answer Key**.

❑ Use **Communipak** Conversations 1–2, pages 101–102, and Tête à tête 1, pages 109–110. Students can prepare floor plans with **Video Activity Book** page 88.

Monitoring and Adjusting

❑ Assign Writing Activities 1–4 in the **Activity Book**, pages 181–182.

❑ Monitor use of place names and directions as students do the practice activities. Refer students to the vocabulary sections on pages 190–194. Use the TEACHING NOTE on page T192 with activity 3.

❑ Do **Teaching to Multiple Intelligences** activities 1 and 2, pages 96–97, to monitor students' understanding of place names.

Assessment

❑ After completing all of the lesson's activities, use Quiz 21 on pages 71–72 of **Lesson Quizzes**. Adjust lesson quizzes to meet students' needs by using the **Test Bank**.

Reteaching

❑ Redo any appropriate activities in the **Activity Book**.

❑ Assign **Teacher to Teacher**, page 12.

❑ Assign portions of the **CD-ROM** or **Video** to reteach parts of the lesson.

Extension and Enrichment

❑ Individual students can use the **CD-ROM** for extension and enrichment.

❑ Use SUPPLEMENTARY VOCABULARY on pages T190, T191, T193, and T194, and the CHALLENGE ACTIVITIES on page T197, to challenge more advanced students.

❑ Have students make a map of their city as described at the bottom of page T193.

❑ Students can choose any one of **Internet Connection Notes** projects 1–4 on pages 55–60 to learn more about various French cities and housing.

Summary and Closure

❑ Help summarize the vocabulary and expressions of the lesson. Then ask students to demonstrate by using **Overhead Visuals** Transparency S13 and the first activity on page A26 or Transparency 32 and the activities on A94, or by describing their house.

❑ Do PORTFOLIO ASSESSMENT on page T196.

End-of-Lesson Activities

❑ *À votre tour!:* Students can prepare and practice activities 1–3, pages 196 and 197. Follow the suggestions at the bottom of page T196 for COOPERATIVE PRACTICE in trios. Assign activities 4 and 5 for written homework.

UNITÉ 6, LEÇON 22: *Weekend à Paris,* PAGE 198

Objectives

Communicative Functions and Topics
To talk about how you get around and modes of transportation

To describe places you often go to

To talk about going to someone's house

To tell what you are going to do

Linguistic Goals
To use the verb *aller* and *aller* + infinitive

To use contractions with *à*

To pronounce semi-vowels /w/ and /j/

To learn the expression *chez*

Cultural Goals
To learn about attractions in Paris and the *métro*

Motivation and Focus

❏   Have students discuss the photos on pages 198–199. Ask them to name their favorite weekend activities and places to visit. Discuss similarities and differences between Paris and local attractions. Share the PHOTO CULTURE NOTES, page T199.

Presentation and Explanation

❏   *Lesson Opener:* Play **Audio** 22.1 or read the opening monologue with students' books closed. Ask students to read page 198 and make a list of the people and the places they go.

❏   *Note culturelle:* Ask students to read *À Paris* on page 199 to find out about some of the places where young people might go on weekends in Paris.

❏   *Grammar A:* Present *aller,* page 200. Model the forms and examples; have students repeat. Explain that *aller* can be used for going someplace or for future activities.

❏   *Grammar B:* Call attention to the preposition *à* and contractions, page 202. Point out the various meanings of *à* and the forms of the contractions.

❏   *Vocabulaire:* Introduce means of transportation using the pictures on **Overhead Visuals** Transparency 33. Model and have students repeat the expressions in the box on page 204. Guide students to talk about places they go, arrival times, and transportation.

❏   *Grammar C:* Explain the use of *chez,* page 205; have students practice talking about going to someone's house. Explain the PRONUNCIATION note, page T205.

❏   *Grammar D:* Introduce the construction *aller* + infinitive, page 206. Model talking about future plans and help students talk about their own plans for the future.

❏   *Prononciation:* Explain semi-vowels, page 207. Model or use **Audio** 22.8 to model pronunciation and have students repeat.

Guided Practice and Checking Understanding

❏   Use **Overhead Visuals** Transparency 33 and the activities on page A95 to practice means of transportation and contractions.

❏   Play **Audio** 22.2–7 or read the **Video Script**, and have students do **Activity Book** activities B–G on pages 169–171.

❏   Use the **Video** or **Video Script** as students do **Video Activity Book** pages 89–93.

❏   Do the TPR activity on page T199 to practice names of places in Paris.

Independent Practice

❑ Do the activities on pages 200–207. Students can work alone on 1, 2, and 6–10. Arrange students in pairs to do 3–5, 7, and 11 as COOPERATIVE PAIR PRACTICE. Have students do activity 12 as homework. Have students check their work with the **Answer Key**.

❑ Use **Communipak** for Conversations 5–8, pages 103–104; Échanges 1–2, pages 105–106; or Tête à tête 2, pages 111–112. Do **Video Activity Book** page 94 to role play brief conversations on the *métro*.

Monitoring and Adjusting

❑ Assign Writing Activities 1–6 on **Activity Book** pages 183–186.

❑ Monitor students as they work on the practice activities. Point out grammar boxes, pages 200–206. Use the TEACHING NOTE: LISTENING ACTIVITIES on page T200, and the ADDITIONAL PRACTICE drill at the bottom of page T202.

❑ Use **Teaching to Multiple Intelligences** activity 3, pages 98–99, to check use of the verb *aller* and the preposition *à*.

Assessment

❑ After students have completed all of the lesson's activities, administer Quiz 22 on pages 73–74 of **Lesson Quizzes**. Adapt questions to meet your needs using the **Test Bank**.

Reteaching

❑ Redo any of the activities in the **Activity Book** for which students need more practice.

❑ Have students do **Teacher to Teacher** pages 13 and 14.

❑ Students can use the **CD-ROM** or **Video** to review portions of the lesson.

Extension and Enrichment

❑ Individual students can use the **CD-ROM** for extension and enrichment.

❑ Share information about other Paris attractions with CULTURAL BACKGROUND: L'OPÉRA, page T203; the PHOTO CULTURE NOTE, page T204; and CULTURAL NOTES, page T206. If students are interested, have them prepare a research project on one of the attractions.

❑ Play the GAME on page T207.

❑ Choose any of the enrichment activities in **Internet Connection Notes** projects 5–9, pages 61–66.

Summary and Closure

❑ Choose one of the lesson's **Communipak** activities that students did not previously do. Have students prepare and practice the exchanges. After students present their work to the class, remind them of the grammar and vocabulary they have learned in the lesson.

❑ Do PORTFOLIO ASSESSMENT on page T208.

End-of-Lesson Activities

❑ *À votre tour!:* Students can prepare and practice activities 1–3, pages 208 and 209. Assign activities 4 and 5 for written homework. Follow the suggestions at the bottom of page T209 for COOPERATIVE READING AND WRITING PRACTICE.

UNITÉ 6, LEÇON 23: *Au Café de l'Univers*, PAGE 210

Objectives

Communicative Functions and Topics
To talk about activities: sports, games, and music
To talk about where people are coming from
To contradict someone
To express surprise

Linguistic Goals
To use stress pronouns and contractions with *de*
To use the verb *venir*
To use the construction noun + *de* + noun
To pronounce vowels /ø/ and /œ/

Cultural Goals
To learn about attractions in Paris and in French cafés

Motivation and Focus

❏ Look at the photos on pages 210–211 and ask the class to imagine they are in the café with friends. What might they talk about? Brainstorm a list of topics.

Presentation and Explanation

❏ *Lesson Opener:* Follow the SETTING THE STAGE suggestions on page T210, listing conversation topics on the board. After listening to **Audio** 23.1, or your reading of the opening text, have students read it and discuss what topics the girls talk about. Make comparisons between the topics students listed and those in the monologue.

❏ *Note culturelle:* Have students read *Au café*, page 211. Encourage them to compare activities in French cafés to their own favorite gathering places.

❏ *Grammar A and B:* Introduce the verb *venir* and the preposition *de*, pages 212–213. Model and have students repeat the forms and examples.

❏ *Vocabulaire:* Present vocabulary for sports, games, and music using the box on page 214. Have students repeat the words and actions. Model the verbs used to talk about sports and music. Encourage students to talk about the sports and musical instruments they play.

❏ *Grammar C:* Introduce stress pronouns, page 215, by following the TEACHING STRATEGY idea in the TE margin. Use **Overhead Visuals** Transparency 16.

❏ *Vocabulary:* Call attention to the expressions for contradicting someone and for expressing surprise, page 216. Encourage students to copy intonation and facial expressions as they practice these phrases.

❏ *Grammar D:* As you present the construction noun + *de* + noun, page 217, use the CRITICAL THINKING suggestion in the TE margin to help students draw conclusions about French word order.

❏ *Prononciation:* Use **Audio** 23.7 or model the text in the box, page 217, to focus students' attention on the vowel sounds /ø/ and /œ/. Have students repeat the words.

Guided Practice and Checking Understanding

❏ Play **Audio** 23.2–6 or read the **Cassette Script** to check listening comprehension with **Activity Book** activities B–F, pages 174–176.

❏ Use the **Video** or **Video Script** as students do **Video Activity Book** pages 95–97.

Independent Practice

❑ Practice vocabulary and structures with the activities on pages 212–217. Students can do activities 2, 3, 7, and 10 for homework. Arrange students in pairs to check their answers together, referring to the **Answer Key** as needed. Model and have students repeat the exchanges in activities 1, 4–6, 8, and 9. Students can then do the activities as COOPERATIVE PAIR PRACTICE, switching roles to allow for more practice.

❑ Use **Communipak** Tête à tête 3, pages 113–114, and Échanges 3–4, pages 107–108, for pair practice in asking and answering questions about sports, music, and games. **Video Activity Book** page 98 can be done in small groups.

Monitoring and Adjusting

❑ Assign **Activity Book** Writing Activities 1–7 on pages 187–190.

❑ Monitor students' language as they work on the activities. Explain the grammar and vocabulary boxes as needed. Use the TOURING PARIS activity, pages T212–T213, to monitor use of ***aller... à***, ***venir... de***, and contractions.

❑ Use **Teaching to Multiple Intelligences** activities 4, 5, and 6, pages 100–106, to monitor names of sports, games, and music, and to stress pronouns.

Assessment

❑ Administer Quiz 23 on pages 75–76 of **Lesson Quizzes** after the lesson's activities are completed. Adapt the test items to your class's needs using the **Test Bank**.

Reteaching

❑ Redo any appropriate activities in the **Activity Book**.

❑ Use the **CD-ROM** and **Video** to reteach portions of the lesson.

Extension and Enrichment

❑ Individual students can use the **CD-ROM** for extension and enrichment.

❑ Students can do CHALLENGE, page T219, to prepare their own illustrated messages. Expand the conversational practice of inviting friends to come along and identifying people by using CHALLENGE, pages T212 and T216. Introduce names of additional sports and musical instruments in SUPPLEMENTARY VOCABULARY, page T214.

❑ Students can explore cyber-cafés and francophone websites on sports and musical instruments with **Internet Connection Notes** projects 10 and 11, pages 67–69.

Summary and Closure

❑ Replay the **Video** for the lesson or have students look back through the lesson in the textbook. Students can work in cooperative groups to make a list of Paris attractions. Encourage students to talk about what places they would like to go to and explain why.

❑ Do PORTFOLIO ASSESSMENT on page T219.

End-of-Lesson Activities

❑ *À votre tour!:* Students can prepare and practice activities 1–3 on page 218. Assign activities 4 and 5 on page 219 for written homework. Follow the suggestions at the bottom of page T218 for COOPERATIVE PRACTICE.

UNITÉ 6, LEÇON 24: *Mes voisins*, PAGE 220

Objectives

Communicative Functions and Topics
To talk about possessions
To identify and describe family members
To express doubt

Linguistic Goals
To use ordinal numbers and possessive adjectives
To indicate possession with *de*
To pronounce vowels /o/ and /ɔ/

Cultural Goals
To learn about places in Paris
To be aware of the popularity of French and American films in France

Motivation and Focus

❑ Ask students to describe the apartment building on page 220. How is this building similar to local homes or apartment buildings? How is it different? Encourage comments on the pictures of buildings on page 221.

Presentation and Explanation

❑ *Lesson Opener:* Use **Overhead Visuals** Transparency 34 with SETTING THE STAGE, pages T220–T221. Play **Audio** 24.1 or read aloud the monologue, page 220. Then ask students to read to determine where the people live in the building.

❑ *Notes culturelles:* Have students read *Versailles* and *La vie en appartement*, page 221. Explain the PHOTO CULTURE NOTE about Versailles in the TE margin.

❑ *Grammar A:* Explain the use of *de* to talk about possessions, page 222. Point out contractions with *de* and have students talk about things possessed by others.

❑ *Vocabulaire:* Introduce family vocabulary, page 223, with **Overhead Visuals** Transparency 8. Model family relationship terms and have students repeat. Then guide students to use the terms to identify family members.

❑ *Grammar B* and *C:* Introduce possessive adjectives. Point out that possessive adjectives need to agree with the nouns they describe. Have students practice the examples on pages 224 and 226. Present the box on expressing a doubt on page 225.

❑ *Grammar D:* Present ordinal numbers, page 227. Model and have students repeat. Point out the LANGUAGE NOTES information in the TE margin.

❑ *Prononciation:* Explain pronunciation of /o/ and /ɔ/ using the ideas in PRONUNCIATION NOTES, page T227. Model or play **Audio** 24.7 and have students repeat the words.

Guided Practice and Checking Understanding

❑ Use **Overhead Visuals** Transparency 8 and the activity on pages A57–A58 to practice describing family members and using possessive adjectives. Practice using ordinal numbers and talking about an apartment building with Transparency 34 and the activities on pages A96–A97.

❑ Use **Audio** 24.3–6 or the **Cassette Script** with **Activity Book** activities C–F, pages 177–180, to check listening comprehension.

❑ Use the **Video** or **Video Script** using pages 99–101 in the **Video Activity Book**.

❑ Practice talking about possession using the TPR activity on page T224.

Independent Practice

❑ Have students do the activities on pages 222–227. Do 1–3, 5, 6, and 9–11 as homework. Model and have students do 4, 7, and 8 as Cooperative pair practice. Have students check their answers with the **Answer Key**.

❑ Use **Communipak** Tête à tête 4, pages 115–116, or **Video Activity Book** page 102 for oral practice about families.

Monitoring and Adjusting

❑ Assign **Activity Book** Writing Activities 1–7 on pages 191–194.

❑ Monitor use of possessive adjectives as students work on the practice activities. Point out the grammar and vocabulary boxes, pages 222–227. Explain the information in Language and Pronunciation notes in the TE margins.

❑ Use **Teaching to Multiple Intelligences** activity 7, pages 107–108, to monitor students' use of possessives.

Assessment

❑ Use Quiz 24 on pages 77–78 of **Lesson Quizzes** after completing the lesson. Give Unit Test 6 (Form A or B) on pages 61–69 of **Unit Tests**. For assessment of specific language skills, select the appropriate **Proficiency Tests**. The **Test Bank** can be used to adjust tests and quizzes to meet the class's specific needs.

Reteaching

❑ Use any appropriate activities from the **Activity Book** for reteaching as necessary.

❑ Assign the **CD-ROM** or **Video** to students for review.

Extension and Enrichment

❑ Individual students may use the **CD-ROM** for extension and enrichment.

❑ Play the Game about possessions on pages T226–T227.

❑ Students can learn more about Versaille, French history, or popular contemporary athletes and films with **Internet Connection Notes** projects 12–15, pages 70–73.

Summary and Closure

❑ Help students summarize the grammar and vocabulary of the lesson. Then show **Overhead Visuals** Transparency 34 and ask them to prepare a short description of one of the families in the picture, using as much of the content of the lesson as possible.

❑ Do Portfolio assessment on page T229.

End-of-Unit Activites

❑ *À votre tour!:* Students can prepare and practice activities 1–3, pages 228 and 229. Assign activities 4 and 5 for written homework.

❑ *Entracte 6:* Follow the Pre- and Post-reading suggestions and teaching tips in the TE margins for *Entracte 6* pages 230–235. Remind them to use cognates as they read.

❑ *Reading and Culture Activities:* Do **Activity Book** pages 195–198.

CULTURAL PHOTO ESSAY: *À Paris*, PAGE 236

Objectives

Cultural Goals To learn about Paris

To recognize major historic and modern attractions

To be aware of various ways of traveling and sightseeing in Paris

Note: You may want to refer back to this Cultural Photo Essay as attractions and travel in Paris are mentioned in later lessons.

Motivation and Focus

❏ Begin the essay by having students look at the photos and maps on the pages 236–243. Encourage them to describe the places and point out landmarks that they have seen before. Encourage students to share any other information they already know about Paris.

❏ As an overview of *À Paris*, play **Video** sections C.1–C.4. Replay it, pausing occasionally to allow students to comment on the sites and sounds of the city. Have students identify and locate the places mentioned in the **Video** on the map on page 237.

Presentation and Explanation

❏ To present important facts about Paris, together read page 236. Check understanding by asking questions. Help students pronounce the names of the attractions. Share information in the PHOTO CULTURE NOTES in the TE margins.

❏ As you present traditional Paris attractions, have students locate them on the map on page 239. Together, read pages 238–239. Guide students to notice the historic and cultural importance of each of the places. Invite students to identify which places they would like to visit. Discuss the CULTURAL BACKGROUND information on page T238.

❏ Ask students to contrast the photos of traditional Paris, pages 238–239, with those of new Paris, pages 240–241. What differences in building style and architectural design do they see? Which do they prefer? Read together about *Le nouveau Paris*, helping students with pronunciation and clarifying information as needed. Discuss the CULTURAL BACKGROUND information, page T240.

❏ Do the PRE-READING activity, page T242, before having students read the letter from Jean-Marc and *Paris en bateau-mouche*, pages 242–243. Check understanding by asking students to summarize the information.

Guided Practice and Checking Understanding

❏ Have students locate the attractions on **Overhead Visuals** Transparency 3, Map of Paris. Invite students to briefly describe each of the places. Then do the POST-READING activity on the bottom of page T242.

❏ As an alternative, describe each of the attractions and have students identify and locate them on the map of Paris, page 237.

Independent Practice

❏ Arrange students in pairs to work on each *Activité culturelle*, pages 239, 241, and 243. Encourage groups to share their responses with the class.

❏ Students can prepare a list of places they would like to visit with the POST-READING activity, page T242. Ask students to explain why they would like to visit the places.

Monitoring and Adjusting

❑ As students read the selections, check understanding by having them locate the places on a map of Paris and explain in their own words why these places are famous.

❑ Use **Overhead Visuals** Transparency 3 to monitor students' listening skills. Say places and have students find them on the map.

Assessment

❑ As an informal assessment of cultural awareness, replay the **Video** without sound and have students identify the places in Paris.

❑ Have students write their responses to each *Activité culturelle* on pages 239 and 241. Check students' writing for accuracy of cultural information and for supporting their choices.

Reteaching

❑ Use **Overhead Visuals** Transparency 3 to reteach sights and attractions of Paris.

❑ To reteach places in Paris, prepare a TPR activity. Place pictures of cards with place names around the classroom. Give instructions for students to go to various places.

Extension and Enrichment

❑ Students can prepare a bulletin board display of Paris. Students may want to prepare a large map, drawings of various attractions, and/or brief descriptions of the attractions.

❑ If students are interested, have them research one of the buildings or places mentioned on pages 236–243. Invite students to share their research results with the class.

❑ Students may want to conduct a poll or survey of favorite Paris attractions. Encourage them to make a graph or chart to display the results.

❑ Students can choose any of the following **Internet Connection Notes** projects about Paris: Unit 3, project 1A, page 21; Unit 5, project 4B, page 46; Unit 6, projects 1A, 2B, 5A, 8A, or 12B, pages 55, 56, 61–62, 65, 70; or Unit 8 long-term projects A or B, pages 101–103.

Summary and Closure

❑ Revisit the map in **Overhead Visuals** Transparency 3. Guide students to name the important sites and buildings in Paris. Encourage students to share what they have learned about Paris geographically, historically, politically, and economically. Summarize its importance as a capital and as a major city in the world.

❑ Alternatively, replay the **Video** for this essay before summarizing the importance of Paris.

UNITÉ 7, LEÇON 25: *L'achat des vêtements,* PAGE 246

Objectives

Communicative Functions and Topics
To talk about clothing, accessories, and stores that sell clothes

To talk about what people are wearing and where to go shopping

To say whether clothes fit and what they look like

To ask for help from a salesperson and find out prices

To use expressions of opinion

To use numbers to 1000 to discuss prices

Linguistic Goals   To use regular *-er* verbs in the present tense

Cultural Goals   To be aware of the French concept of style

Motivation and Focus

❏ Students can identify the type of stores and clothing in the photos on pages 244–245. Ask about their favorite places to buy clothes and the types of clothes they like. Discuss the importance of clothes and style. Read *Thème et Objectifs* on page 245 to preview content of the unit.

❏ Introduce **Interdisciplinary/Community Connections** Project Seven on pages 64–66, and help students begin to plan their projects.

Presentation and Explanation

❏ *Lesson Opener:* Ask students to identify the types of stores in the photos on pages 246–247. Use SETTING THE STAGE, page T246, to find out students' favorite shopping places. Have them read the captions about the types of stores, encouraging comments on similarities and differences between their favorite stores and those in the photos. Read *Accent sur...,* page 246. Use CRITICAL THINKING SKILLS, page T247, to point out French words used in fashion.

❏ *Vocabulary A:* Use **Overhead Visuals** Transparency 35 to introduce clothes, page 248. Model the clothing items and have students repeat, play **Audio** 25.1, or read the **Cassette Script**, page 34. Explain the LANGUAGE NOTES, page T248. Students can identify clothing they are wearing.

❏ *Vocabulary B:* Introduce accessories, page 250, with **Overhead Visuals** Transparency 36, following the same procedure with **Audio** 25.2 or the **Cassette Script**, page 34.

❏ *Vocabulary C:* Present vocabulary and expressions for getting help from a salesperson and discussing clothes with a friend, page 252. Use **Overhead Visuals** Transparency 37 to clarify meaning. Students can repeat the words and expressions.

Guided Practice and Checking Understanding

❏ Use the activities suggested on pages A98–A102 of **Overhead Visuals** with Transparencies 35–37 to practice clothing vocabulary.

❏ Check students' listening comprehension with **Audio** 25.1–6 or **Cassette Script** pages 34–35, and **Activity Book** activities A–F on pages 203–205.

❏ Have students do **Video Activity Book** pages 103–107 as they watch **Video** Module 5 or listen as you read the **Video Script**, pages 51–52.

❏ Do the TPR activity with clothing on page T248.

Independent Practice

❏ Do the oral practice activities on pages 249–253 for homework. Then arrange students in pairs for COOPERATIVE PAIR PRACTICE with exercises 1, 4, and 7–8. Have pairs check their work with the **Answer Key**.

❏ Use any of **Communipak** Interviews 1–4, pages 121–122, Conversations 1–2, pages 125–126, Échange 1, page 129, or Tête à tête 1, pages 133–134, for additional practice with clothing vocabulary. **Video Activity Book** page 108 is suitable for small-group work.

Monitoring and Adjusting

❏ Assign Writing Activities 1–4 in the **Activity Book**, pages 219–222.

❏ Monitor listening skills with SUPPLEMENTARY LISTENING PRACTICE, page T249. Use the suggestions for EXPANSION and VARIATION activities on pages T249 and T251 to challenge more advanced students.

❏ Check knowledge and use of clothing vocabulary with **Teaching to Multiple Intelligences** activities 1 and 2, pages 109–110.

Assessment

❏ Use Quiz 25 on pages 79–80 of **Lesson Quizzes** after students have completed the lesson's activities. You can adapt the questions to the class's specific needs with the **Test Bank**.

Reteaching

❏ Redo any appropriate activities in the **Activity Book**.

❏ Use **Teacher to Teacher** pages 18–19 to reteach clothing items.

❏ Assign portions of the **CD-ROM** to reteach parts of the lesson or for make-up work, or have students watch the **Video**.

Extension and Enrichment

❏ Individual students can use the **CD-ROM** for extension and enrichment.

❏ Play the GAME, page T252, with **Overhead Visuals** Transparency 12. Do the CHALLENGE activity: UNE IDOLE on page T253. See the SUPPLEMENTARY VOCABULARY lists, pages T248 and T250, for additional clothing and store items.

❏ Students can choose one of the research activities about clothing stores in **Internet Connection Notes** projects 1–3, pages 75–78.

Summary and Closure

❏ Use Transparency S15 and the suggestions at the bottom of page A29 of **Overhead Visuals** to summarize vocabulary and expressions used in shopping for clothes.

❏ Use the suggestions for PORTFOLIO ASSESSMENT on page T255.

End-of-Lesson Activities

❏ *À votre tour!*: Students can prepare and practice activities 1–4, pages 254–255. Follow the suggestions at the bottom of the TE page for COOPERATIVE PRACTICE with activities 1–4. Assign written self-expression activities 5 or 6 for homework.

UNITÉ 7, LEÇON 26: *Rien n'est parfait!*, PAGE 256

Objectives

Communicative Functions and Topics
To talk about clothing and accessories and describe what clothes look like

To talk about where to buy clothes

To emphasize a remark

Linguistic Goals
To use the verbs *mettre*, *acheter*, and *préférer*, the demonstrative *ce*, and the interrogative *quel?*

To pronounce the letters "*e*" and "*è*"

Cultural Goals
To learn about French department stores

Motivation and Focus

❏ Use the WARM-UP AND REVIEW activity, page T256, with **Overhead Visuals** Transparency 38 to review clothing items and prices.

❏ Have students brainstorm a list of questions to consider before buying clothes. Students can look at the photos on pages 256–257 for some ideas: size, color, price.

Presentation and Explanation

❏ *Lesson Opener:* Play **Video** or **Audio** 26.1, or act out the scenes on pages 256–257. Replay with students repeating. Have them read the conversations silently; then discuss the clothing Frédéric is thinking about buying and why he doesn't buy it.

❏ *Note culturelle:* Read and discuss *Le grand magasin*, pages 256–257. Share the PHOTO CULTURE NOTE on page T257.

❏ *Grammar A:* Present the verbs on page 258, pointing out accent changes. Introduce other verbs with the same patterns in the *Vocabulaire* box, page 259.

❏ *Grammar B:* Explain use and forms of the demonstrative adjective *ce*, page 260. Introduce the expression **Eh bien!**, page 260, and have students practice using it.

❏ *Grammar C:* Introduce the forms of the interrogative adjective *quel*, page 261. Show how they are used with various nouns to ask questions.

❏ *Grammar D:* Present the forms of the irregular verb *mettre*, page 262. Ask students to repeat the forms, pointing out the silent "t" in singular forms.

❏ *Prononciation:* Explain and model the pronunciation of the letters "*e*" and "*è*," page 263. Play **Audio** 26.6 and have students practice the sounds of the vowels.

Guided Practice and Checking Understanding

❏ Practice verb forms with **Overhead Visuals** Transparency 16 and the suggestions on page A67. Use Transparency 38 and the activities on pages A103–A104 to practice numbers 100–1000, *ce* and *quel*, and *préférer* and *acheter*.

❏ Use the **Audio**, **CD-ROM**, or **Cassette Script** to check listening skills as students do **Activity Book** activities C–E on pages 208–209.

❏ Check understanding of the opening text with *Compréhension* on page 257. Replay the **Video** for the entire lesson, or read the **Video Script**, and have students complete the activities on pages 109–111 of the **Video Activity Book**.

Independent Practice

❑ Practice new vocabulary and grammatical constructions with the activities on pages 258–263. Students can work alone or do activities 1–3 and 7–9 for homework. Have students check their work with the **Answer Key**. Ask students to work in pairs to do activities 4–6 as COOPERATIVE PAIR PRACTICE activities.

❑ In pairs, have students prepare Échange 2, page 130, of **Communipak**. Invite pairs to present their conversations to the class. Students can play the game on page 112 of the **Video Activity Book** to practice forms of *ce* and *quel*.

Monitoring and Adjusting

❑ Assign the Writing Activities in the **Activity Book** on pages 223–226.

❑ Monitor students' use of the lesson's structures as they work on the practice activities. Refer them to the grammar explanations on pages 258–262 as needed. Refer to TEACHING STRATEGIES and LANGUAGE NOTES in the TE margins for further explanations. Use LISTENING ACTIVITY: PRéFéRENCES, page T261, to monitor understanding of interrogative adjective forms.

❑ Use the **Writing Template** and **Teaching to Multiple Intelligences** activities 3 and 4, pages 111–112, to monitor students' use of the structures of this lesson.

Assessment

❑ After students have completed all of the lesson's activities, administer Quiz 26 on pages 81–82 of **Lesson Quizzes**. Use the **Test Bank** to adjust the questions to your class's needs.

Reteaching

❑ Have students redo activities in the **Activity Book** that correspond to structures or functions that students find difficult.

❑ Students can use the **CD-ROM** to review portions of the lesson or for make-up work.

Extension and Enrichment

❑ Individual students can use the **CD-ROM** for extension and enrichment.

❑ Play the game described in the TEACHING NOTE on page T262.

❑ Students can choose one of the enrichment activities in **Internet Connection Notes** projects 4–6, pages 79–81.

Summary and Closure

❑ Use Transparency S15 and the suggestions on the bottom of page A29 of **Overhead Visuals** to summarize the lesson's vocabulary and structures.

❑ Do PORTFOLIO ASSESSMENT on page T265.

End-of-Lesson Activities

❑ *À votre tour!:* Have students practice activities 1–3, pages 264–265, in pairs. Students can use the **Answer Key** to check their conversations. Invite pairs to present their exchanges to the class. Assign the composition, activity 4 on page 265, for homework.

UNITÉ 7, LEÇON 27: *Un choix difficile*, PAGE 266

Objectives

Communicative Functions and Topics
To describe actions
To describe people and things (new, beautiful, old)
To express comparisons
To introduce an opinion
To decide what to choose

Linguistic Goals
To use regular *-ir* verbs
To use comparisons
To pronounce the letters "*ill*"

Cultural Goals
To learn about how French young people buy clothes

Motivation and Focus

❏ Have students describe what is happening in the photos on pages 266–267. Talk about where they prefer to do their clothes shopping: small stores/boutiques or department stores. Ask about occasions for wearing formal clothes. What types of occasions are formal? What types of clothing are appropriate? Where can you buy formal clothing?

❏ Do SETTING THE SCENE, page T266, to introduce **Audio** or **Video** section 27.1. As an alternative, read **Video Script** 27.1, page 55, or **Cassette Script** 27.1, page 36.

Presentation and Explanation

❏ *Lesson Opener:* Dramatize the text or replay the **Audio**. Ask students to read the conversations silently and then summarize what is happening.

❏ *Note culturelle:* Have students read *Le choix de vêtements* on page 266. Encourage them to compare shopping habits of French and American young people. Play the **Video** or **CD-ROM** for 27.4, Vignette culturelle: Dans un centre commercial, or read the **Video Script** on page 56 to present information about a French commercial center.

❏ *Grammar A:* Present regular *-ir* verbs, page 268. Point out endings and have students repeat. Use **Overhead Visuals** Transparency 39 to introduce other *-ir* verbs.

❏ *Grammar B:* Model describing people and things using **Overhead Visuals** Transparency 40 with the adjectives *beau*, *nouveau*, and *vieux*. Point out the placement of the adjectives before the nouns in the examples on page 269.

❏ *Grammar C:* Present the constructions used in comparisons on page 270. Model examples using students and objects in the class. Introduce the expression *à mon avis*..., page 271, to talk about personal opinions.

❏ *Prononciation:* Explain the pronunciation of the letters "*ill*" on page 271. Play **Audio** 27.5, asking students to listen for the sound. Replay and have students repeat.

Guided Practice and Checking Understanding

❏ Follow the suggestions in **Overhead Visuals**, pages A103–A107, with Transparencies 16 and 38–40 to practice comparisons, *-ir* verbs, and adjectives. You may also use WARM-UP AND REVIEW: TELLING TIME, page T268, and Transparency 6.

❏ Play the **Audio** or read the **Cassette Script**, and have students do **Activity Book** activities A–D, pages 211–213.

❏ Use the questions in *Compréhension* on page 267 to check students' understanding of the opening text. Students can do pages 113–115 in the **Video Activity Book** as they watch the **Video**, or listen as you read the **Video Script**.

❏ Use the TPR activity, pages T270–T271, to monitor understanding of comparatives.

Independent Practice

❏ Do the activities on pages 268–271. Assign activities 1–4 and 6–7 for homework. Have students check their answers with the **Answer Key**. Model and have students repeat activities 5 and 8 before arranging them in pairs for COOPERATIVE PAIR PRACTICE.

❏ Use **Communipak** Échange 3, page 131, Tête à tête 2–3, pages 135–138, or **Video Activity Book** page 116 for pair practice in making comparisons.

Monitoring and Adjusting

❏ Students can do the Writing Activities on pages 227–230 of the **Activity Book**.

❏ Monitor students' use of **-ir** verbs and adjectives as they do the practice activities. Point out grammar and vocabulary boxes as needed. Use the TEACHING STRATEGIES on pages T268 and T271.

❏ Use **Teaching to Multiple Intelligences** activity 5, page 113, to monitor students' understanding of comparatives.

❏ Use the **Writing Template** to monitor use of this lesson's structures and functions.

Assessment

❏ For formal assessment of the lesson, use Quiz 27 on pages 83–84 of **Lesson Quizzes**. The **Test Bank** can be used to modify test items to meet a particular class's needs.

Reteaching

❏ Redo activities from the **Activity Book** as appropriate to help with items that students find difficult.

❏ Reteach **-ir** verbs, comparisons, and vocabulary with **Teacher to Teacher** pages 20–21.

Extension and Enrichment

❏ To challenge students, introduce the SUPPLEMENTARY VOCABULARY, page T268, and do the EXPANSION suggestions, page T269.

❏ Use the **Internet Connection Notes** projects 7–8 on pages 82–83.

Summary and Closure

❏ Use Transparency S16 and the activities on pages A31–A32 of **Overhead Visuals** to help students summarize what they have learned about comparisons and **-ir** verbs.

❏ Do PORTFOLIO ASSESSMENT on page T273.

End-of-Lesson Activities

❏ *À votre tour!:* Have students do activities 1 and 4 for homework. They can check their own answers, using the **Answer Key** or listening to the **Audio** as needed. Do activities 2 and 3 in small groups. Have students write their personal responses to activity 5.

UNITÉ 7, LEÇON 28: *Alice a un job,* PAGE 274

Objectives

Communicative Functions and Topics
To talk about where to go shopping, what you need, what you like

To use money-related expressions and find out prices

To give advice and indicate approval

To give commands

Linguistic Goals
To use regular *-re* verbs and the verb *payer*

To use the pronoun *on* and the imperative

To pronounce the letters "*an*" and "*en*"

Cultural Goals
To learn about the ways in which young people earn money

Motivation and Focus

❑ Have students preview the photos on pages 274–275. Encourage comments about the jobs pictured. Compare the jobs in the photos to local jobs that young people have.

❑ Use WARM-UP AND REVIEW, page T274, with **Overhead Visuals** Transparency 20 to practice vocabulary.

Presentation and Explanation

❑ *Lesson Opener:* Together, read the introductory paragraph, page 274. Play the **Video** or **Audio** 28.1, or model the opening conversation, pausing to check comprehension. Ask students to read the dialogue and discuss its content.

❑ *Note culturelle:* Ask students to read *L'argent de jeunes,* page 275. Compare work opportunities for French and American young people.

❑ *Vocabulaire:* Introduce money vocabulary on page 276. Model using the words and expressions. Have students create other questions and sentences using the vocabulary.

❑ *Grammar A:* Explain the pronoun *on* on page 278. Show how it is used in general statements with third-person singular verb forms.

❑ *Grammar B:* Present regular *-re* verbs on page 280. Introduce other *-re* verbs with **Overhead Visuals** Transparency 41.

❑ *Grammar C:* Model giving commands using the imperative on page 281. Point out affirmative and negative forms.

❑ *Prononciation:* Explain the pronunciation of "*an*" and "*en*" on page 283. Play **Audio** 28.8 and have students repeat the words and sentences.

Guided Practice and Checking Understanding

❑ Use the activities on **Overhead Visuals** pages A108–A109 and Transparencies 16 and 41 to practice *-re* verbs.

❑ Check listening comprehension with **Activity Book** activities C–G on pages 216–218. Play **Audio** 28.2–8 or read **Cassette Script** pages 38–39 for the activities.

❑ Play **Video** Module 28 or read the **Video Script** as students complete **Video Activity Book** pages 117–121.

Independent Practice

❑ Model the activities on pages 276–283. Assign activities 3–5, 8–11 and 14 for homework. Have students use the **Answer Key** to check their work. Model and have students practice activities 1, 2, 6, 7, 12–13, and 15 as COOPERATIVE PAIR PRACTICE.

❏ Use any of the following for pair practice: **Communipak** Tu as la parole 1–6, pages 123–124, or Conversations 2–8, pages 125–128; or **Video Activity Book** page 122.

Monitoring and Adjusting

❏ Assign the Writing Activities in the **Activity Book** on pages 231–234.
❏ Monitor use of **-re** verbs and the imperative as students work on practice activities. Point out grammar and vocabulary boxes, pages 276–281. Explain information in LANGUAGE NOTES and PRONUNCIATION NOTES, pages T279–T283. Use TEACHING STRATEGIES on pages T280 and T282 to explain verb endings.
❏ Do **Teaching to Multiple Intelligences** activities 6–7, pages 114–115, to reteach regular **-re** verbs.
❏ Use the **Writing Template** to monitor use of this lesson's vocabulary and structures.

Assessment

❏ Use Quiz 28 on pages 85–86 of **Lesson Quizzes** after students have completed the lesson. Administer Unit Test 7 (Form A or B) on pages 70–78 of **Unit Tests** as a comprehensive assessment of the unit. You may also do any or all of the **Proficiency Tests** for the unit.
❏ Use Comprehensive Test 2 (Form A or B) on pages C-29–C-56 of **Comprehensive (Semester) Tests** to assess Units 5–7.

Reteaching

❏ Redo appropriate activities from the **Activity Book**.
❏ Assign the **CD-ROM** or **Video** for review or for make-up work.

Extension and Enrichment

❏ Individual students can use the **CD-ROM** for extension and enrichment.
❏ Play the GAME: DRILLING WITH DICE, pages T282–T283, for more practice with verb forms.
❏ Students can learn more about jobs, attitudes toward money, or classified ads by doing **Internet Connection Notes** projects 9–13, pages 84–88.

Summary and Closure

❏ As pairs of students present any of the **Communipak** activities for this unit, have the rest of the class summarize functions and structures that have been learned.
❏ Do PORTFOLIO ASSESSMENT on page T285.

End-of-Unit Activities

❏ *À votre tour!:* Have students prepare activities 2–4 on pages 284–285 and then do them as COOPERATIVE PRACTICE. They can use the **Audio** or **Answer Key** to check their responses. Have students practice writing advice in activity 5, page 285.
❏ *Entracte 7:* Use the suggestions in the TE margins to read and discuss the selections on pages 286–291.
❏ *Reading and Culture Activities:* Assign **Activity Book** pages 235–237.

UNITÉ 8, LEÇON 29: *Le weekend et les vacances*, PAGE 296

Objectives

Communicative Functions and Topics   To discuss common weekend activities, summer and winter sports, and French holidays

To discuss leisure activities: going out with friends, sports

To talk about household chores and helping around the house

To describe vacation travel plans: travel dates, how to travel, how long to stay

Linguistic Goals   To use *faire de* + sport

Cultural Goals   To learn about popular weekend and sports activities in France

Motivation and Focus

❑   Ask students to turn to pages 294–295 and identify activities in the photos of the *Unit Opener*. Students can talk about their favorite leisure activities. What do they like to do? Where would they like to go for weekends or on vacation? Read together *Thème et Objectifs* to preview the unit.

❑   Introduce the **Interdisciplinary/Community Connections** project on pages 67–69. Break students into groups and help them begin to plan their unit projects.

Presentation and Explanation

❑   *Lesson Opener:* Have students read the photo captions on pages 296–297. Students can read *Accent sur...*, page 296, for homework. In class, have them summarize the information about French teenagers' favorite leisure activities. Use the suggestions in CROSS-CULTURAL COMPARISONS, page T297, to compare to the class's favorites.

❑   *Vocabulary A:* Do the WARM-UP AND REVIEW on page T298. Introduce weekend activities using **Overhead Visuals** Transparency 42. Point out the vocabulary and expressions in the box on page 298. Students can talk about their plans for the weekend using the new words and expressions.

❑   *Vocabulary B:* Model and present language for discussing vacations and sports activities, pages 300–301. Use Transparency 43 to introduce sports. Have students repeat the expressions as they mime actions for each of the sports. Ask students to identify their favorite winter and summer sports.

❑   *Note culturelle:* Ask students to read *Le calendrier des fêtes françaises* on page 301, and find the French holidays on a calendar. Share the PHOTO CULTURE NOTES about the holidays in the TE margin. Students can point out holidays that are similar in both France and in the U.S., and holidays (or dates of holidays) that are different.

Guided Practice and Checking Understanding

❑   Use **Overhead Visuals** Transparencies 42 and 43 and the activities on pages A110–A113 to practice the vocabulary presented in this lesson.

❑   Play the **Audio** or read **Cassette Script** pages 40–41 as students do Listening Comprehension Activities A–E in the **Activity Book**, pages 243–246.

❑   Use the **Video**, or read **Video Script** pages 59–60, with **Video Activity Book** pages 123–127. Go over the answers with the class.

❑   Do the TPR activity about sports on page T300.

Independent Practice

❏ Do the activities on pages 299 and 302–303 for homework. Explain that the direction lines at the beginning of each activity are now given in French (see the TEACHING NOTE on page T299). Students can write their responses to activities 3, 4, and 6. Do activity 4 as COOPERATIVE GROUP PRACTICE, page T302, and activity 6 as COOPERATIVE PAIR PRACTICE.

❏ Use **Communipak** Tu as la parole 1–3, page 147, for additional pair practice. Students can also work in small groups on **Video Activity Book** page 128.

Monitoring and Adjusting

❏ Assign the Writing Activities on pages 259–260 of the **Activity Book**.

❏ As students work on the practice activities, monitor use of new vocabulary. Have students study the vocabulary boxes on pages 298–301 as needed. Explain forms of the verb *nettoyer* with the TEACHING STRATEGY on page T298. Use the suggestions for VARIATION, EXPANSION, and CHALLENGE activities for more advanced students.

❏ Use **Teaching to Multiple Intelligences** activity 1, pages 116–117, to monitor students' understanding of weekend, vacation, and sports activities.

❏ Use the **Writing Template** to monitor use of leisure time expressions.

Assessment

❏ Administer Quiz 29 on pages 87–88 of **Lesson Quizzes** after all the lesson's activities are completed. Use the **Test Bank** to adjust the lesson quiz to the class's specific needs.

Reteaching

❏ Redo any appropriate activities from the **Activity Book**.

❏ Assign portions of the **CD-ROM** or **Video** to reteach parts of the lesson.

Extension and Enrichment

❏ Individual students may use the **CD-ROM** for extension and enrichment.

❏ Play the GAME about leisure activities on page T301. Use the CHALLENGE: CONVERSATIONAL ROLE PLAY on page T305 as a follow-up to students' compositions on vacation plans. Introduce SUPPLEMENTARY VOCABULARY for sports and holidays on page T300. Use the REALIA NOTES to help students read the vacation advertisements on pages T300 and T305.

❏ If students are interested, have them choose one of the **Internet Connection Notes** projects on pages 91–93 about leisure activities and vacations.

Summary and Closure

❏ Use **Overhead Visuals** Transparency S17 and the activities on pages A33–A34 to help students summarize what they have learned about favorite weekend and vacation activities.

❏ Do PORTFOLIO ASSESSMENT on page T305.

End-of-Lesson Activities

❏ *À votre tour!:* Have students do activities 1 and 2 on page 304 as COOPERATIVE PRACTICE (page T304), checking their answers in the **Answer Key**. Assign WRITTEN SELF-EXPRESSION activity 3, page 305, for homework.

UNITÉ 8, LEÇON 30: *Vive le weekend!*, PAGE 306

Objectives

Communicative Functions and Topics
To talk about how you and others feel
To narrate what did and did not happen in the past, and talk about sequence

Linguistic Goals
To use expressions with *avoir*
To use the *passé composé* of *-er* verbs
To pronounce the letters "*ain*" and "*in*"

Cultural Goals
To compare French and American concepts of weekend

Motivation and Focus

❏ Have students identify activities in the pictures on pages 306–307. Ask students to talk about favorite activities and to describe what they did last weekend.

❏ Use SETTING THE SCENE, page T306. Play **Video** 30.1–2 or read **Video Script**, page 61, using gestures to convey meaning. Ask students to recall Jean-Claude's activities.

Presentation and Explanation

❏ *Lesson Opener:* Play **Audio** 30.1, or read **Cassette Script** page 41, to model the opening monologue with books closed. Replay, having students repeat. Ask them to read the *Lesson Opener* on page 306; talk about past weekend activities with *Et toi?*, page 307.

❏ *Note culturelle:* Ask students to read *Le weekend*, page 307. Use **Video** 30.6 or the **Video Script** to present additional information about teenagers' interest in movies. Do the CROSS-CULTURAL OBSERVATION on page T307.

❏ *Vocabulary A:* Use the WARM-UP: QUEL ÂGE AS-TU?, page T308. Introduce expressions with *avoir*, page 308, with **Overhead Visuals** Transparency 44. Model the expressions and have students repeat several times.

❏ *Grammar B:* Present the *passé composé* of *-er* verbs, page 309. Model the examples; have students repeat. Explain that this tense is used to describe past actions.

❏ Model sequencing words; have students repeat the examples in the box on page 311.

❏ *Grammar C:* Explain negative with *passé composé*, page 312. Model and have students repeat. Have students talk about things that did not happen in the past.

❏ *Grammar D:* Introduce questions in the past, page 314. Model the examples; have students repeat. Point out questions with intonation, *est-ce que*, and inversion.

❏ *Prononciation:* Model pronunciation of the letters "*ain*" and "*in*," page 315. Play **Audio** 30.7 and have students repeat the words and sentence.

Guided Practice and Checking Understanding

❏ Use **Overhead Visuals** Transparency 44 with the suggestions on page A115 to practice *avoir*. The *passé composé* can be practiced with Transparencies 14a and b, 17, and 42, using activities on pages A64, A68, and A111.

❏ Check students' listening comprehension with **Audio** 30.2–6 or **Cassette Script** pages 41–42 and **Activity Book** activities C–G, page 247–249.

❏ Students can do **Video Activity Book** pages 129–133 as they watch the **Video** or listen to you read the **Video Script**, pages 61–62.

❏ Use the TPR activity on page T309 to practice past activities.

Independent Practice

❏ Model the activities on pages 308–315. For homework students can do activities 1–3, 6, 7, 9–11, and 13. Have them check their work using the **Answer Key**. Do activities 4–5, 8, 12, 14, and 15 as cooperative pair practice.

❏ Students can work in pairs to practice communicative skills with **Communipak** Échange 1, page 153; Tu as la parole 4–6, page 148; or Conversations 1 and 4, pages 149–150. In groups, students can work on a survey on **Video Activity Book** page 134.

Monitoring and Adjusting

❏ Have students complete **Activity Book** activities 1–7 on pages 261–264.

❏ Monitor students as they work on the activities. Use TEACHING STRATEGIES and LANGUAGE NOTES, pages T308–T315, to explain vocabulary and grammar.

❏ Use **Teaching to Multiple Intelligences** activities 2 and 3, pages 118–121, to monitor expressions with *avoir* and use of the *passé composé*.

❏ The **Writing Template** can be used to monitor production.

Assessment

❏ Use Quiz 30 on pages 89–90 of **Lesson Quizzes** after students have completed all of the lesson's activities. You may modify questions to meet individual needs with the **Test Bank**.

Reteaching

❏ Redo any appropriate activities from the **Activity Book**. Students can also use the **CD-ROM** or **Video** to review portions of the lesson.

❏ Do **Teacher to Teacher** page 23 to reteach *avoir* expressions.

Extension and Enrichment

❏ Individual students may use the **CD-ROM** for extension and enrichment.

❏ Play the game about last Saturday on page T310. Students may also prepare role plays using the SUPPLEMENTARY VOCABULARY, page T317.

❏ Students can choose to do **Internet Connection Notes** project 5, page 94.

Summary and Closure

❏ Use **Overhead Visuals** Transparency S17 and the second activity on page A34 to help students summarize what they have learned about talking about past events.

❏ Do PORTFOLIO ASSESSMENT on page T317.

End-of-Lesson Activities

❏ *À votre tour!:* Students can work individually on activities 2 and 6, pages 316–317. Do 1 and 3 as COOPERATIVE PRACTICE, page T316. Have students choose one of the role plays in activities 4–5 and work in pairs to prepare, practice, and present it to the class.

UNITÉ 8, LEÇON 31: *L'alibi,* PAGE 318

Objectives

Communicative Functions and Topics	To identify periods of future and past time
	To describe vacation plans: how long to stay and what to see
	To narrate what you did and didn't do
Linguistic Goals	To use the verb *voir*
	To use the *passé composé* of *-ir, -re*, and irregular verbs
	To pronounce the letter "*gn*"
Cultural Goals	To learn about how French young people spend their weekends and leisure time

Motivation and Focus

❑ Ask students to relate something good and something bad that happened to them recently. Use SETTING THE SCENE, page T319, and play **Video** 31.1, or read **Video Script** page 63, using drawings and gestures to clarify meaning. Guide students to recall the unfortunate events that happened to Philippe and the happy ending.

Presentation and Explanation

❑ *Lesson Opener:* Play **Audio** 31.1, or read **Cassette Script** page 43. to present the opening text. Ask students to read page 318; follow the suggestions for COOPERATIVE READING, page T318.

❑ *Note culturelle:* Tell students to read *Les jeunes Français et la télé*, page 319. Help them describe typical TV viewing habits of French young people. Encourage students to compare French viewing habits with their own. Play the **Video** or read **Video Script** 31.4 on pages 63–64.

❑ *Grammar A:* Introduce the verb *voir* and guide students to use the forms to talk about what one sees, page 320. Model the verb forms. Point out that it is irregular.

❑ *Grammar B:* Explain how to form the *passé composé* with regular *-ir* and *-re* verbs, page 321. Model the examples and have students repeat both affirmative and negative forms.

❑ *Grammar C:* Present irregular verbs in the *passé composé*, page 323. As students study the verbs, point out the LANGUAGE NOTE in the TE margin. Help students with pronunciation as they repeat the examples in the grammar box.

❑ *Vocabulaire:* Model time expressions for the various tenses in the box on page 324. Use a calendar to clarify meanings as needed. Encourage students to use the time expressions to talk about when events happened in the present, past, and future.

❑ *Prononciation:* Students can listen to **Audio** 31.6 to focus attention on the pronunciation of the letters "**gn**." Model the examples, page 325, as students repeat.

Guided Practice and Checking Understanding

❑ Use **Overhead Visuals** Transparencies 39 and 41 with the activities on pages A105 and A108 to practice past forms of *-ir* and *-re* verbs.

❑ Play the **Audio** or read the **Cassette Script** as students do **Activity Book** activities B–E, pages 252–253, to check listening comprehension skills.

❑ Students can complete **Video Activity Book** pages 135–139 as they watch **Video** 31.1–4 or listen to you read the **Video Script**.

❑ Use the TPR activity, pages T322–T323, to practice past and present verb tenses.

Independent Practice

❏ Model the activities on pages 320–325. Assign 1–4, 6, 10, 12, and 13 for homework. Have students check their answers with the **Answer Key**. Do 5, 7, 8, 9, and 11 as COOPERATIVE PAIR PRACTICE.

❏ Use **Communipak** Échanges, 1 and 2 on pages 153–154 and Tête à tête 1 and 2, pages 157–160, or **Video Activity Book** page 140.

Monitoring and Adjusting

❏ Assign the Writing Activities on **Activity Book** pages 265–266.

❏ Monitor use of past forms of *-ir*, *-re*, and irregular verbs as students work on the practice activities. Point out grammar and vocabulary boxes. Use TEACHING STRATEGIES, LANGUAGE NOTES, and VARIATIONS, pages T320–T323, for additional practice as needed.

❏ The **Writing Template** may be used to monitor production of past-time narratives.

Assessment

❏ Administer Quiz 31 on pages 91–92 of **Lesson Quizzes** after the lesson's activities are completed. Use the **Test Bank** to adapt questions to your class's particular needs.

Reteaching

❏ Redo any activities from the **Activity Book** that students found difficult.

❏ The **CD-ROM** or the **Video** may be used to reteach specific portions of the lesson.

Extension and Enrichment

❏ Individual students may use the **CD-ROM** for extension and enrichment.

❏ Play the game MOI AUSSI on pages T324–T325. You may also use the CHALLENGE ACTIVITY on page T318 and SUPPLEMENTARY VOCABULARY on page T324 for more advanced students.

❏ Students can explore French TV and Paris attractions with **Internet Connection Notes** projects 6–8, pages 95–97.

Summary and Closure

❏ As a culminating activity, have pairs of students present any **Communipak** activities. As a class, check and summarize usage of the *passé composé*.

End-of-Lesson Activities

❏ *À votre tour!:* Do activities 1 and 3, page 326, as COOPERATIVE PRACTICE (see page T326). Have students share their responses to activity 2 with the class. Arrange students in pairs to prepare and present a role play, activity 4 or 5, page 327. Have students write their personal responses to activity 6.

UNITÉ 8, LEÇON 32: *Qui a de la chance?*, PAGE 328

Objectives

Communicative Functions and Topics	To discuss things you never do
	To narrate where you went and when you returned
	To remain vague about certain details
Linguistic Goals	To use *ne ... jamais*
	To use the *passé composé* with *être*
	To use *quelqu'un* and *quelque chose* and their opposites
	To pronounce the letters "*qu*"
Cultural Goals	To be aware of weekend and leisure time activities in the French-speaking world

Motivation and Focus

❑ Introduce the lesson by playing **Video** 32.4 or reading **Video Script** page 66 to act out the *Vignette culturelle*. Have students identify the types of music mentioned.

❑ Ask students about their music preferences. What's their favorite type of music? Favorite musical group? Do they listen to music on the radio? On CD? At live concerts?

Presentation and Explanation

❑ *Lesson Opener:* Present the opening text, page 328, by playing **Audio** 32.1 or reading **Cassette Script** 32.1 on page 45 as students follow in their books. Replay, pausing to check comprehension. Have students do the COOPERATIVE READING activity, page T328.

❑ *Note culturelle:* Read the *Les jeunes Français et la musique*, page 329. Ask students to identify music items mentioned. Have them discuss their own feelings about music.

❑ *Grammar A:* Do WARM-UP AND REVIEW, pages T330–T331. Introduce the *passé composé* of *aller*, page 330. Have students repeat the examples in the grammar box. Point out other verbs that use *être* in the past with the *Vocabulaire* box, page 332.

❑ *Grammar B:* Explain the construction *ne... jamais*, used to talk about never doing something, page 334. Model the examples and have students repeat the forms.

❑ *Grammar C:* Present expressions used to identify people and things, page 335. Model and have students repeat.

❑ *Prononciation:* Model pronunciation of the letters "*qu*." Use **Audio** 32.6 and have students repeat the words and expressions in the box, page 335.

Guided Practice and Checking Understanding

❑ Use the *Compréhension* and *Et toi?* activities on page 329 to check understanding of the opening text and to have students talk about places they went last weekend.

❑ Use **Overhead Visuals** Transparency 42 and the third Review and Practice activity on page A111 to practice the *passé composé* with *être*.

❑ Play the **Audio** or read the **Cassette Script** as students complete Listening Comprehension Activities B–E in the **Activity Book**, pages 255–257.

❑ Play the **Video** for the lesson as students do pages 141–145 of the **Video Activity Book**.

❑ Do the TPR activity on pages T332–T333.

Independent Practice

❑ Model the activities on pages 331–335. Have students do activities 1, 3, and 5–9 alone or for homework, and 2, 4, and 10 as COOPERATIVE PAIR PRACTICE.

❑ Choose any of the following **Communipak** activities for additional practice: Interviews 1–8, pages 143–146; Conversations 5–8, pages 151–152; Échange 3, page 155; Tête à tête 3–4, pages 161–164. You may also do **Video Activity Book** page 146.

Monitoring and Adjusting

❑ Assign Writing Activities 1–6 in the **Activity Book**, pages 267–270.

❑ Monitor students as they practice. Point out the grammar and vocabulary boxes on pages T330–T335. Use the NOTES and TEACHING STRATEGIES In the TE margins.

❑ Use **Teaching to Multiple Intelligences** activity 7 on pages 126–129 to monitor the *passé composé* with *être*.

❑ The **Writing Template** can be used to monitor students' production.

Assessment

❑ Use Quiz 32 on pages 93–94 of **Lesson Quizzes** after students have completed all of the lesson's activities. Adapt questions to your class's needs with the **Test Bank**.

❑ Administer Unit Test 8 (Form A or B) on pages 79–87 of **Unit Tests**. For additional assessment of specific language skills, select any or all of the **Proficiency Tests** for the unit.

Reteaching

❑ Redo appropriate activities from the **Activity Book**. Reteach past tense with *être* by using the VARIATION and EXTRA PRACTICE ideas, pages T332–T333.

❑ Assign the **CD-ROM** or **Video** for reteaching.

Extension and Enrichment

❑ Individual students can use the **CD-ROM** for extension and enrichment.

❑ Students can research French music, attractions, and vacation sites with **Internet Connection Notes** activities 9–11 and the long-term projects, pages 98–103.

Summary and Closure

❑ Use **Overhead Visuals** Transparency S18 and the activity at the bottom of page A35 to help students summarize what they have learned about narrating past events.

❑ Do PORTFOLIO ASSESSMENT on page T337.

End-of-Unit Activities

❑ *À votre tour!:* Do the activities on pages 336–337. Do 1 and 3 as COOPERATIVE PRACTICE. Have pairs role play 2, 4, or 5. Have students practice writing questions in activity 6.

❑ *Entracte 8:* Do pages 338–343. See PRE- and POST-READING notes on the TE pages. Have students use context clues and cognates to guess meanings of new words. Discuss REALIA, PHOTO CULTURE NOTES, and NOTES CULTURELLES on the TE pages.

❑ *Reading and Culture Activities:* Have students do **Activity Book** pages 271–274.

UNITÉ 9, LEÇON 33: *Les repas et la nourriture,* PAGE 346

Objectives

Communicative Functions and Topics
To talk about meals, place settings, foods, beverages, fruits, and vegetables

To express food preferences

To make a shopping list, interact with vendors, and ask prices

Linguistic Goals To use quantity expressions

Cultural Goals To learn about French meals and grocery shopping habits

Motivation and Focus

❏ Discuss the photos on pages 344–345. Ask students to compare meals and stores in the photos to those in the U.S. Share PHOTO CULTURE NOTES, page T345. Read together *Thème et Objectifs*, noting the variety of language used to talk about food.

❏ Ask students to read *Accent sur...*, pages 346–347. Encourage them to use the photos to make cross-cultural comparisons about meals. Explain the CULTURAL NOTES and PHOTO CULTURE NOTES in the TE margins. Do USING THE VIDEO on page T346 to preview the lesson.

❏ Introduce the **Interdisciplinary/Community Connections** project on pages 70–72 and help students begin planning how to create a cookbook in French.

Presentation and Explanation

❏ *Vocabulary A:* Present meals, page 348, and help students talk about times, places, and preferences for each of the meals. Explain the LANGUAGE NOTE about **la cuisine**, page T348. Use **Overhead Visuals** Transparency 45 to introduce table settings. Model vocabulary and have students repeat several times. Share the information in the CULTURAL NOTE in the TE margin.

❏ *Vocabulary B:* Introduce food and beverage vocabulary, pages 350–351, using the TEACHING STRATEGY on the bottom of page T350 with **Overhead Visuals** Transparencies 46a and b. Students can practice talking about food preferences. Encourage them to notice cognates with the CRITICAL THINKING activity, page T351.

❏ *Vocabulary C:* Present fruits and vegetables, pages 354–355, with **Overhead Visuals** Transparencies 47 and 48. Have students repeat the vocabulary. Point out quantity expressions. Students can use the vocabulary and expressions to talk about shopping for food and to practice asking for quantities of food from a merchant.

❏ *Note culturelle:* Have students read *Le marché* on page 355 and compare it to what they know about American supermarkets and markets. Share the information in the CULTURAL NOTES on page T355.

Guided Practice and Checking Understanding

❏ Practice food vocabulary with the activities suggested on pages A116–A123 of **Overhead Visuals**, using Transparencies 45–48.

❏ Play **Audio** 33.1–5 or read **Cassette Script** page 48 as students do Listening Comprehension Activities A–E on **Activity Book** pages 279–281.

❏ Play **Video** 33.1–6, or read **Video Script** pages 67–68, while students do **Video Activity Book** pages 147–151.

❏ Do the TPR activity on table setting on page T348, and the one on fruits and vegetables on pages T354–T355.

Independent Practice

❏ Model and have students practice the vocabulary and communicative expressions in the activities on pages 349–355.

❏ Then arrange students in pairs for the COOPERATIVE PAIR PRACTICE of activities 3–7, 11, and 12. Students may use the **Answer Key** to check their work.

❏ Use any of the following pair practice activities in **Communipak**: Tu as la parole 1–4 on page 172; Conversations 1 and 3 on pages 175–176; or Tête à tête 1 on pages 183–184. In addition, students can role play a customer and fruit vendor with **Video Activity Book** page 152.

Monitoring and Adjusting

❏ Assign **Activity Book** Writing Activities 1–5 on pages 295–298.

❏ As students work on the practice activities, monitor their use of vocabulary. Have them study the vocabulary boxes on pages T348–T355 as needed.

❏ Monitor students' understanding of food and meal vocabulary with activity 1 in **Teaching to Multiple Intelligences**, page 130.

❏ The **Writing Template** can be used to monitor production of the lesson's vocabulary.

Assessment

❏ After students have completed all of the lesson's activities, administer Quiz 33 on pages 95–96 of **Lesson Quizzes**. You can use the **Test Bank** to adjust lesson quizzes to students' needs.

Reteaching

❏ Reteach meals and menus with COOPERATIVE GROUP PRACTICE, page T353, or **Teacher to Teacher**, page 24.

❏ Students can use the **CD-ROM** or **Video** to review portions of the lesson.

Extension and Enrichment

❏ Introduce SUPPLEMENTARY VOCABULARY, pages T348, T350–T351, and T355. Discuss the CULTURAL and REALIA NOTES in the TE margins, pages T348–T357.

❏ If students are interested, have them choose one of the **Internet Connection Notes** projects on pages 105–107 to learn more about French foods, meals, and food stores.

Summary and Closure

❏ Use **Overhead Visuals** Transparency S20 and the activities on pages A39–A40 to role play shopping. Guide students to summarize vocabulary used for food shopping.

❏ Do PORTFOLIO ASSESSMENT on page T357.

End-of-Lesson Activities

❏ *À votre tour!:* Have students work individually on activities 1–4, pages 356–357. Follow the TEACHING STRATEGY on page T356 and the suggestions at the bottom of that page for COOPERATIVE PRACTICE with activities 1 and 4.

UNITÉ 9, LEÇON 34: *À la cantine,* PAGE 358

Objectives

Communicative Functions To identify foods and beverages
and Topics To talk about what you can, should, and want to eat
Linguistic Goals To use the verbs *vouloir*, *p rendre*, and *boire*
To use partitive articles
To pronounce the letters "*ou*" and "*u*"
Cultural Goals To compare French and American cafeterias and food selections

Motivation and Focus

❏ Use the suggestions for SETTING THE SCENE on page T358 and the photos on pages 358–359 to discuss school cafeterias. How do French cafeterias compare to school cafeterias in the U.S.? What food is served? What similarities and differences do students see?

❏ Preview the lesson with **Video** 34.1 and 34.5, or read the **Video Script** on pages 69–70. Explain the scenes as noted at the bottom of page T359. Encourage discussion and comments.

Presentation and Explanation

❏ *Lesson Opener:* Play **Audio** 34.1, or read the **Cassette Script**, page 49, to model the opening conversation. Have students read page 358 and discuss what is being said.

❏ *Note culturelle:* Read and discuss *À la cantine,* page 359. Explain the PHOTO CULTURAL NOTE and CULTURAL NOTES, page T359. Compare cafeteria menus and talk about favorite foods.

❏ *Grammar A:* Present the irregular verb forms of *vouloir*, page 360. Model the expressions and have students repeat. Point out that students have already studied *je* and *tu* forms to talk about food and activity preferences in *Lessons 9* and *13*.

❏ *Grammar B:* Introduce *p rendre* and other verbs with similar conjugations, page 361. Help with pronunciation of the forms, page T361. Students can use the new verbs to talk about food they have, things they learn, and things they do (or don't) understand.

❏ *Grammar C and D:* Explain partitive articles, page 362. Compare whole items and parts of items with **Overhead Visuals** Transparency 49. Introduce partitive forms used in negative sentences, page 365. Model and have students repeat the examples.

❏ *Grammar E:* Point out the irregular verb *boire*, page 367. Guide students to use the forms to talk about different beverages they drink at meals.

❏ *Prononciation:* Use the box on page 367 to point out the letters "*ou*" and "*u*" in words that students know. Use **Audio** 34.8 to model and have students pronounce the words.

Guided Practice and Checking Understanding

❏ Check students' understanding of the opening conversation with *Compréhension* on page 358. Encourage students to talk about their school meals with *Et toi?* on page 359.

❏ Practice verb forms with **Overhead Visuals** Transparencies 16 and 33 and pages A67 and A95; practice the partitive with Transparency 49 and page A124.

❏ Use **Audio** 34.1–7 or **Cassette Script** pages 49–50 for listening comprehension practice with **Activity Book** activities C–G, pages 283–285.

❏ After students have viewed the **Video** for the lesson, or listened to **Video Script** pages 69–70, do **Video Activity Book** pages 153–157.

❏ Do the TPR activities CHOOSING FOODS and DRINKING BEVERAGES, pages T361 and T367.

Independent Practice

❑ Model the activities on pages 360–367. Students can work alone or do 1–6, 8–10, 12, 17 and 18 for homework and check their answers with the **Answer Key**. Arrange students in pairs for COOPERATIVE PAIR PRACTICE of activities 7, 11, and 13–16.

❑ Select appropriate **Communipak** activities: Interviews 1–6, pages 169–171; Échanges 1 and 2, pages 179–180; Tête à tête 2, pages 185–186. You may also do the information gap activity in the **Video Activity Book**, page 158.

Monitoring and Adjusting

❑ Assign the Writing Activities on pages 299–302 of the **Activity Book**.

❑ As students work on the activities, monitor their language use. Point out grammar explanations, pages 360–367. Use LANGUAGE NOTES and other marginal notes, pages T360–T365, to explain vocabulary and reinforce grammar points, and the TEACHING STRATEGY on page T362 for partitives. Use the TEACHING STRATEGY, page T367, to help pronounce "*u*."

❑ Do **Teaching to Multiple Intelligences** activity 2, pages 131–133, for further practice with *p rendre* and the partitive articles.

Assessment

❑ Use Quiz 34 on pages 97–98 of **Lesson Quizzes** after students have completed all of the lesson's activities. Adapt test questions to your class's needs with the **Test Bank**.

Reteaching

❑ Redo any appropriate activities from the **Activity Book**.

❑ Use the TEACHING PROJECT, page T364, to reteach food and beverage vocabulary with *p rendre* and *boire*.

❑ Students can use the **CD-ROM** or **Video** to review portions of the lesson.

Extension and Enrichment

❑ Individual students can use the **CD-ROM** for extension and enrichment.

❑ Have students practice partitives with the games on pages T365 and T366.

❑ Students can choose one of the enrichment activities in **Internet Connection Notes** projects 4–6, pages 108–109.

Summary and Closure

❑ Read **Video Script** 34.1 and 34.5, or replay the **Video**. Review and summarize what students have learned about French food, irregular verbs, and the partitive.

❑ Do PORTFOLIO ASSESSMENT on page T369.

End-of-Lesson Activities

❑ *À votre tour!:* Have students work individually on activities 1–2, page 368, checking their work with the **Audio** or **Answer Key**, and in pairs on activity 3. Do the role plays in 4–5, page 369, in pairs. Assign activity 6 for homework.

UNITÉ 9, LEÇON 35: *Un client difficile*, PAGE 370

Objectives

Communicative Functions and Topics
To talk about what you can, should, and want to eat
To ask others to help you plan a meal
To eat out with friends and talk about people you know
To ask for service

Linguistic Goals
To use the verbs *pouvoir* and *devoir*
To use pronouns *me*, *te*, *nous*, and *vous*
To use pronouns with commands
To pronounce the letters "*s*" and "*ss*"

Cultural Goals
To learn about French restaurants and cuisine

Motivation and Focus

❏ Have students look at the photos on pages 370–371 and discuss what is happening.

❏ Students can share experiences they have had in restaurants and with ethnic foods. Help them identify common French foods.

Presentation and Explanation

❏ *Lesson Opener:* Present the dialogue on page 370 with **Video** 35.1, **Audio** 35.1, or by reading the **Video** or **Cassette Script**. Ask students to read the page and retell the events. Encourage them to talk about comic restaurant situations they have experienced.

❏ *Note culturelle:* Students can compare French and American cuisine after reading the cultural note on page 371. Help with pronunciation of borrowed French words by following the TEACHING STRATEGY in the TE margin. Explain the PHOTO CULTURE NOTES.

❏ *Grammar A:* Introduce object pronouns, page 372. Point out the form and placement. Model and have students repeat. Point out the verbs related to doing things for people, page 373. Mime actions of helping people and have students choose the correct verbs.

❏ *Grammar B:* Present giving orders with object pronouns, page 374. Point out the change in position and form in affirmative and negative imperative statements.

❏ *Grammar C:* Present the irregular verbs *pouvoir* and *devoir*, page 376. Guide students to note similarities in forms between *pouvoir* and *vouloir*. Point out forms students have already studied with REVIEW AND EXPANSION, page T376.

❏ *Prononciation:* Help students distinguish between "*s*" and "*ss*." Model or use **Audio** 35.6 to model the words in the box on page 377. Have students repeat several times.

Guided Practice and Checking Understanding

❏ Do the *Compréhension* and *Et toi?* activities on page 371 to check understanding of the opening text and to encourage students to talk about their own personalities.

❏ Use **Audio** 35.3–4, or read the **Cassette Script**, with **Activity Book** activities B–D, pages 287–289, to practice listening comprehension.

❏ Have students complete **Video Activity Book** pages 159–163 as they watch the **Video** or listen to the **Video Script**.

❏ Use the TPR activity on page T374 to practice use of object pronouns.

Independent Practice

❏ Model the activities on pages 372–377. Students can in pairs practice activities 1, 2, 5, 8, and 10. Assign activities 3–4, 6–7, 9, and 11–12 for homework. Go over the answers with the class or have students check their own work with the **Answer Key**.

❏ Use any of these activities from **Communipak** for additional oral practice: Tu as la parole 5 and 7, page 173; or Tête à tête 3, pages 187–188. Use **Video Activity Book** page 164 to have students role play visiting and bringing things to a sick friend.

Monitoring and Adjusting

❏ Monitor understanding with the Writing Activities in the **Activity Book**, pages 303–306.

❏ Monitor use of object pronouns and the verbs **pouvoir** and **devoir** as students do the activities. Point out grammar and vocabulary boxes. Use Variations, Expansion, Teaching strategies, Teaching notes, and Language notes on pages T372 –T376.

❏ Use **Teaching to Multiple Intelligences** activity 3 on pages 134–135 to monitor vocabulary and activity 4 on pages 136–137 to monitor pronunciation.

❏ Monitor production of the lesson's structures and vocabulary with the **Writing Template**.

Assessment

❏ Administer Quiz 35 on pages 99–100 of **Lesson Quizzes** after the lesson's activities are completed. Adapt the quiz items to your class's needs with the **Test Bank**.

Reteaching

❏ Redo any activities in the **Activity Book** that cause difficulty.

❏ Use **Teacher to Teacher** page 25 to reteach the verbs **pouvoir** and **devoir**.

❏ The **CD-ROM** or the **Video** may be used to reteach portions of the lesson.

Extension and Enrichment

❏ Individual students may use the **CD-ROM** for extension and enrichment.

❏ Do Making crêpes on page T370. Encourage students to describe how to prepare a favorite food.

❏ If students are interested, have them explore restaurants around the world and Cajun cuisine with **Internet Connection Notes** Internet Project 7, page 110.

Summary and Closure

❏ Use **Overhead Visuals** Transparency S19 and the second activity on page A38 to have students role play dialogues using vocabulary and structures from this lesson.

❏ Do Portfolio assessment on page T379.

End-of-Lesson Activities

❏ À votre tour!: Do activities 1 and 3, page 378, as Cooperative practice (page T378). Assign the role plays in activities 4 and 5, page 379, as pair activities. Students can write their own responses in activity 6.

UNITÉ 9, LEÇON 36: *Pique-nique*, PAGE 380

Objectives

Communicative Functions and Topics To ask the waiter/waitress to bring things for others
To talk about what others have said or written

Linguistic Goals To use the verb *connaître*, *dire*, and *écrire*
To use pronouns *le*, *la*, *les*, *lui*, and *leur*
To pronounce the letters "*on*" and "*om*"

Cultural Goals To learn about French picnics and vacation spots

Motivation and Focus

❏   Have students look at the photos on pages 380–381 and discuss what the people might be saying. You may wish to show **Video** 36.1 and 36.4, or read the **Video Script**, to introduce the lesson. Share information in PHOTO CULTURE NOTES in the TE margins.

❏   Do SETTING THE SCENE, page T380, to begin discussion of picnics. Students may work in small groups to brainstorm a list of picnic places, foods, and beverages.

Presentation and Explanation

❏   *Lesson Opener:* Play **Audio** 36.1, or read the **Cassette Script** for the opening text, pages 380–381. Have students read and discuss the conversation.

❏   *Grammar A:* Present *connaître*, page 382. Point out the irregular forms. Guide students to use *connaître* to talk about people and places they know.

❏   *Grammar B:* Introduce direct object pronouns, page 383. Point out forms and position in sentences. Help students begin to use the direct object pronouns.

❏   *Grammar C:* Point out placement of direct object pronouns in imperative statements, page 385. Compare placement in affirmative and negative commands.

❏   *Grammar D:* On page 386, explain use of indirect object pronouns *lui* and *leur*. Have students note forms and placement. Point out the verbs on page 387 that are commonly followed by indirect object pronouns. Model and have students repeat the examples.

❏   *Grammar E:* Present the irregular verbs *dire* and *écrire* on page 388. Point out the forms of each. Model the examples and guide students to use the verbs.

❏   *Prononciation:* Play **Audio** 36.7 and have students practice the sounds in the box on page 389. Explain the information in the TE margin.

Guided Practice and Checking Understanding

❏   Do the *Compréhension* and *Et toi?* activities on page 381 to check understanding of the opening conversations and to guide students to talk about their own picnics.

❏   **Activity Book** activities C–F, pages 291–292, can be used with **Audio** 35.3–6 or the **Cassette Script** for listening practice.

❏   After viewing the **Video**, or listening to the **Video Script**, students can complete pages 165–167 of the **Video Activity Book**.

❏   Use the TPR activity on pages T382–T383 for additional practice.

Independent Practice

❏   Do the practice activities on pages 382–389. Activities 1, 2, 6, 10, and 12–15 can be done individually or as homework. Students can check their work in the **Answer Key**. Model and have students do activities 3–5, 7–9, and 11 as COOPERATIVE PAIR PRACTICE.

❏ Do any of **Communipak** Conversations 2, 4, 5, and 6, pages 175–178, Tu as la parole 6 and 8, page 173, or Échanges 3 and 4, pages 181–182. For additional pair practice, use **Video Activity Book** page 168.

Monitoring and Adjusting

❏ Assign the Writing Activities in the **Activity Book**, pages 307–311.

❏ Monitor use of pronouns and verb forms. Point out grammar and vocabulary boxes, pages 382–388. Use the TEACHING STRATEGIES, LANGUAGE NOTES, VARIATIONS, EXTRA PRACTICE, and EXPANSION suggestions in the TE margins through page T389.

❏ Use **Teaching to Multiple Intelligences** activities 5–7 on pages 138–144 to reteach pronunciation and verbs *connaître*, *dire*, and *écrire*.

❏ Use the **Writing Template** to monitor students' production of the lesson's objectives.

Assessment

❏ Use Quiz 36 on pages 101–102 of **Lesson Quizzes** after students have completed the lesson. Questions can be adapted to a class's particular needs with the **Test Bank**.

❏ Administer Unit Test 9 (Form A or B) on pages 88–96 of **Unit Tests** as a comprehensive assessment of the unit. Assess specific language skills with any of the unit **Proficiency Tests**.

Reteaching

❏ Redo appropriate activities from the **Activity Book** as necessary.

❏ Have students use the **CD-ROM** or **Video** to review portions of the lesson.

Extension and Enrichment

❏ Individual students can use the **CD-ROM** for extension and enrichment.

❏ Students can research national parks and recreation areas or local cafés and restaurants with **Internet Connection Notes** Internet Project 8, pages 111–112.

Summary and Closure

❏ Have pairs of students redo one of the role plays in **Communipak** and present it to the class. The rest of the class can summarize communicative objects for the lesson.

End-of-Unit Activities

❏ *À votre tour!:* Do any or all of the activities on pages 390–391. Students can use the **Audio** or **Answer Key** to check responses to activities 1 and 3. Have pairs of students role play activities 2, 4, and 5. Have students write descriptions of people in activity 6.

❏ *Entracte 9:* Help with the reading selections on pages 392–397 by using the PRE-READING and POST-READING suggestions throughout. Encourage students to use cognates and context clues. Discuss the PHOTO CULTURE and REALIA NOTES on pages T392–T396. Assign the writing activity on page 395.

❏ *Reading and Culture Activities:* Do **Activity Book** activities A–E on pages 313–317.

SAMPLE LESSON PLANS

HEATH

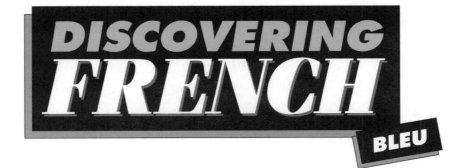

DISCOVERING FRENCH

BLEU

Dr. Teresa Carrera-Hanley
McDougal Littell

Pamela Knapp
Kingswood Regional High School
Wolfeboro, New Hampshire

David Miller
Davis High School
Kaysville, Utah

McDougal Littell
Evanston, Illinois • Boston • Dallas

Contents

Introduction ....S/v

UNITÉ 1 Bonjour!   *Dr. Teresa Carrera-Hanley*

Leçon 1 La rentrée S2
Leçon 2 Tu es français? S5
Leçon 3 Salut! Ça va? S7
Leçon 4 Le français pratique: L'heure S10

UNITÉ 3 Bon appétit!   *Pamela Knapp*

Leçon 9 Tu as faim? S14
Leçon 10 Au café S18
Leçon 11 Ça fait combien? S21
Leçon 12 Le français pratique: Le temps S24

UNITÉ 4 Qu'est-ce qu'on fait?   *David Miller*

Leçon 13 Le français pratique: Mes activités S32
Leçon 14 Qui est là? S36
Leçon 15 Une boum S40
Leçon 16 Une interview...S44

UNITÉ 7 Le shopping   *Pamela Knapp*

Leçon 25 Le français pratique: L'achat des vêtements S50
Leçon 26 Rien n'est parfait! S56
Leçon 27 Un choix difficile S62
Leçon 28 Alice a un job S68

Additional Lesson Plan Blank Forms S78

© D.C. Heath and Company, a Division of Houghton Mifflin Company

Introduction

DISCOVERING FRENCH is a *flexible* program that provides a wide range of teaching options. Since lesson planning is a highly individual activity, this flexibility allows teachers to build their own curriculum. It must take into account the individual needs and differences of both students and teachers, and focus on the skills and topics relevant to each. These plans are not specific as to methodology, only as to the organization and presentation of the program resources.

The sample lesson plans that follow offer suggestions and possible options for presenting the material in DISCOVERING FRENCH: you will certainly have your own "customized" approach designed to accommodate *your* particular classroom needs. In fact, we have provided forms for convenient annotation on pages 77–86.

Your Extended Teacher's Edition also presents general pacing guidelines on pages 44–45 as well as on-page pacing suggestions for each unit.

© D.C. Heath and Company, a Division of Houghton Mifflin Company

Description

There are four sample lesson plans contained in this booklet. They are designed to address both traditional and block scheduling needs.

Sample lesson plans for *block scheduling,* prepared by Dr. Teresa Carrera-Hanley, are found on pages 2–13. Block scheduling offers an excellent opportunity to use a variety of teaching tools such as video and CD-ROM in small group work. (See pages 50–51 in your Extended Teacher's Edition for a general discussion of cooperative learning and practice.)

An alternate approach to *block scheduling,* based on 90-minute class periods meeting every other day, is found on pages 32–48, prepared by Dave Miller. These plans are based on his actual teaching plans. He uses bell quizzes each day immediately following the tardy bell to get his students to class on time, to help them focus on French right away and to review the previous class session's material. Because his main

© D.C. Heath and Company, a Division of Houghton Mifflin Company

teaching goal is oral proficiency, he uses the textbook activities primarily for paired-student oral practice.

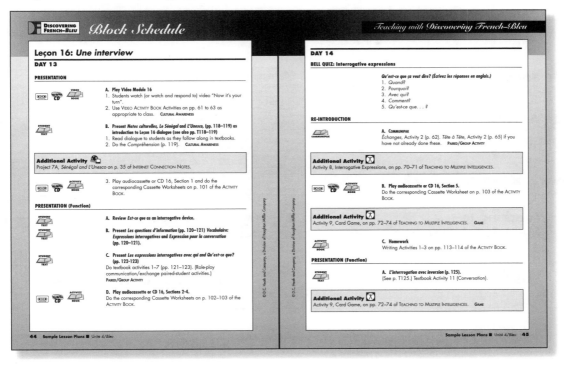

Lesson plans for shorter class periods were prepared by Pamela Knapp. These are found on pages 14–30 and 50–77.

© D.C. Heath and Company, a Division of Houghton Mifflin Company

The following icons are used throughout the Lesson Plans to denote different components being used.

 Student Text

 Communipak

 Activity Book

Video Activity Book

Teacher's Resource Package (TRP)

Teaching to Multiple Intelligences

Interdisciplinary/Community Connections

Teacher to Teacher

Internet Connection Notes

 Overhead Transparencies

Videodisc

 Videocassette

Audiocassette

CD-ROM

Audio CD

 Portfolio Assessment

Unit Testing

```
ASSESSMENT OPTIONS
  Portfolio
  Assessment
PROFICIENCY TESTS
  Listening Comprehension      Reading
  Performance Test             Performance Test
  Speaking                     Writing
  Performance Test             Performance Test
  Unit Test          Test Bank
  (Achievement)      (Computerized)
  CD-ROM  Cahier, Exploration
```

Lesson Quizzes

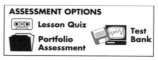
```
ASSESSMENT OPTIONS
  Lesson Quiz
  Portfolio              Test
  Assessment             Bank
```

© D.C. Heath and Company, a Division of Houghton Mifflin Company

There is also a regular item called **Additional Activities**. These do not necessarily fit into the allotted time, but are activities, games or drills from other components of **DISCOVERING FRENCH** that may be used at that point in the lesson sequence to help teach particular words or functions.

Additional Activity 1
Les nourritures Have fun practicing food vocabulary with the drill *Les nourritures* on p. 43 of TEACHING TO MULTIPLE INTELLIGENCES. **GAME** ❖ **PAIRED/GROUP ACTIVITY** ❖ **PERSONALIZATION**

Additional Activity 2
Les nourritures Have students do Internet Project 1 on p. 21 of INTERNET CONNECTION NOTES using the Web to find their favorite snacks in Paris! **PERSONALIZATION** ❖ **TECHNOLOGY**

Additional Activity 3
Au restaurant Have students interview each other using p. 39 of the COMMUNIPAK. They will take each other's orders in a French restaurant!

The **DISCOVERING FRENCH** program can be comfortably adapted to any lesson plan. You and your students will discover a wealth of options in its practical approach to proficiency, including integrated technology for each lesson, an emphasis on daily life themes, cooperative learning, and self-expression.

© D.C. Heath and Company, a Division of Houghton Mifflin Company

Sample Lesson Plans

UNITÉ 1 Bonjour! *by Dr. Teresa Carrera-Hanley*
Leçon 1: *La rentrée*

DAY 1

| | | ANSWER KEY Answers to Student Text and COMMUNIPAK activities. |

TEACHING RESOURCES	TIME	STRATEGIES
1. Warm-up: Listening comprehension STUDENT TEXT	**15 min.**	Transition to French. Greetings and introductions. Practice listening comprehension with the 3 mini-conversations on p. 14 of the textbook and the *Pour Communiquer* section on p. 15. Use Overhead Transparencies S3 and S4, *La rentrée* and *Bonjour!* to illustrate greetings and *la rentrée*. **MULTIPLE INTELLIGENCES: SPATIAL ❖ CRITICAL THINKING ❖ CULTURAL AWARENESS**

Additional Activity
Students will enjoy working on the project The First Day of School on pages 45–47 of INTERDISCIPLINARY/COMMUNITY CONNECTIONS.

| **2. Listening comprehension: *La rentrée***
  | **25 min.** | Play all of Video Module 1 as an introduction to the lesson. Provide students copies of VIDEO ACTIVITY BOOK copymasters, pp. 1–4, and replay the video. Have your students work in pairs on these activities for more comprehension and understanding. Play the audiocassette and do the Activity Book Cassette worksheets, pp. 3–5. **PAIRED/GROUP ACTIVITY ❖ MULTIPLE INTELLIGENCES: SPATIAL ❖ CRITICAL THINKING ❖ CULTURAL AWARENESS** |
| **3. Reading comprehension and cultural awareness**
 STUDENT TEXT | **5 min.** | Students read the *Notes Culturelles* on p. 15 of the textbook to themselves. Use the TE cross-cultural observation suggestion to develop culture awareness. Read the *Petit commentaire* on Astérix on p. 16. Ask students to do their own cross-cultural observation by comparing Astérix with a popular American cartoon character. **CULTURAL AWARENESS** |

Additional Activity
If your school has Internet access, make use of it for your French class with TRP component INTERNET CONNECTION NOTES, Project 1, p. 1, and Project 2, p. 3, where they can find Astérix in action!

© D.C. Heath and Company, a Division of Houghton Mifflin Company

TEACHING RESOURCES	TIME	STRATEGIES
4. Speaking proficiency: Introductions and greetings	**15 min.**	Do activities 1–4 on p. 16 of the textbook. Use the chain activity suggested in the ETE. Use Overhead Transparency S4, *Bonjour!* CULTURAL AWARENESS ❖ PERSONALIZATION ❖ PAIRED/GROUP ACTIVITY

Additional Activity

Have students do Internet Project 4 in TRP component INTERNET CONNECTION NOTES (p. 8) for more ways to say hello.

TEACHING RESOURCES	TIME	STRATEGIES
5. Accents	**5 min.**	Teach *Les signes orthographiques* on p. 17 of the textbook. See Language notes (T17).
6. Numbers 0–10	**10 min.**	Introduce numbers 0-10. Follow TPR suggestions on p. T17. Use audiocassette Lesson 1, Section 4. TPR ❖ MULTIPLE INTELLIGENCES: BODILY-KINESTHETIC ❖ MULTIPLE INTELLIGENCES: MUSICAL

Additional Activity

Let students play a game to practice numbers using *Les nombres de 0 à 10* on page 12 of TEACHING TO MULTIPLE INTELLIGENCES.

TEACHING RESOURCES	TIME	STRATEGIES
7. French alphabet	**15 min.**	Introduce the French alphabet. Do modeling and repetition. Have class work in pairs saying the alphabet. Ask students to spell their first and last name in French. PAIRED/GROUP ACTIVITY ❖ PERSONALIZATION

Additional Activity

Use art work and TPR in *L'alphabet* on page 10 of TEACHING TO MULTIPLE INTELLIGENCES.

© D.C. Heath and Company, a Division of Houghton Mifflin Company

TEACHING RESOURCES	TIME	STRATEGIES
Homework ACTIVITY BOOK STUDENT TEXT		ACTIVITY BOOK: Writing Activities pp. 19–20. Study: *Pour communiquer* vocabulary on p. 15 of the textbook. Pair work: Learn to spell your name in French. Be ready to spell the name of a famous American person for a classroom partner. **MULTIPLE INTELLIGENCES: LINGUISTIC ❖ PAIRED ACTIVITY ❖ PERSONALIZATION**

Additional Activity CD-ROM

If you have access to a computer with CD-ROM, combine suggestions 6 and 7 above and ask students to work in trios with the DISCOVERING FRENCH INTERACTIVE, CD-ROM, Part A, Lesson 1 for about 25 minutes. If you have only one computer in your classroom, set up learning stations and ask a group of students to work with the DISCOVERING FRENCH INTERACTIVE, BLEU, Part A. The other groups can work on learning numbers and the alphabet or even playing the game *Le pendu* as suggested on p. T16 of the textbook. Students take turns working at the various learning stations.

© D.C. Heath and Company, a Division of Houghton Mifflin Company

Leçon 1: *La rentrée*/Leçon 2: *Tu es français?*

DAY 2

TEACHING RESOURCES	TIME	STRATEGIES

1. Warm-up: Speaking proficiency

STUDENT TEXT

20 min.

Check homework. Ask students to work in pairs and check the accuracy of their responses as they do speaking assignment with partner.
Optional game: Have 10 small pieces of paper with the last names of 10 students. Spell one at a time aloud and ask, **«Qui est-ce?»**. Student whose name is spelled should raise a hand.
Ask students to read the *Petit commentaire* on p. 16 of the textbook and be ready to say their favorite cartoon character and spell the name in French. **PAIRED/GROUP ACTIVITY**
❖ **PERSONALIZATION** ❖ **MULTIPLE INTELLIGENCES: BODILY-KINESTHETIC**
❖ **GAME** ❖ **CULTURAL AWARENESS**

---

2. Listening comprehension and speaking proficiency: Nationalities

VIDEODISC   CD-ROM
VIDEO BOOK   STUDENT TEXT

20 min.

Greet students around the room and introduce nationalities by asking where they are from. Use Overhead Transparency 4, *Les nationalités*, to discuss nationalities. Teach *Pour communiquer* on page 19 of the textbook. Show Video Module 2, *Tu es français?* Give students copies of Module 2 pp. 5–8 of the VIDEO ACTIVITY BOOK and replay video mini-scenes. Use self-expression and group activity for pp. 7–8 of the VIDEO ACTIVITY BOOK.
CULTURAL AWARENESS ❖ **SELF-EXPRESSION** ❖ **COOPERATIVE LEARNING** ❖
PERSONALIZATION ❖ **MULTIPLE INTELLIGENCES: MUSICAL**

Additional Activity
Have groups of students make collages and play a game with them in *Les nationalités*, pages 13 and 14 in TEACHING TO MULTIPLE INTELLIGENCES.

---

3. Adjective agreement

STUDENT TEXT

15 min.

Teach the adjective agreement of nationalities on p. 19 of the textbook. Ask students to do Activities 1, 2 and 3 on pp. 20-21 in pairs. **PAIRED/GROUP ACTIVITY**

© D.C. Heath and Company, a Division of Houghton Mifflin Company

Block Schedule

TEACHING RESOURCES	TIME	STRATEGIES
4. Numbers *CD* / STUDENT TEXT	**15 min.**	Review numbers 0–10 and teach numbers 10–20. Use audiocassette, Unit 1, Lesson 2, Section 3. Do Activity 4, *La fusée Ariane*, on p. 21 of the textbook, in groups. Do TPR activity with numbers 11–20 on p. T21. **TPR** ❖ **COOPERATIVE LEARNING** ❖ **MULTIPLE INTELLIGENCES: MUSICAL** ❖ **REVIEW**
5. Pronunciation: *les lettres muettes* *CD* / STUDENT TEXT	**5 min.**	Practice pronunciation, p. 21 of the textbook. Play audiocassette Lesson 2, Section 4. Read the *Petit commentaire* on p. 20 of the textbook. **MULTIPLE INTELLIGENCES: MUSICAL** ❖ **CULTURAL AWARENESS**
6. Writing proficiency: Introductions, greetings and nationalities ACTIVITY BOOK	**10 min.**	Assign students Writing Activities 1–3 on pp. 21–22 of the ACTIVITY BOOK in class. After they finish their individual work, have students work in pairs to check the accuracy of their responses. **PAIRED/GROUP ACTIVITY** ❖ **CULTURAL AWARENESS**
7. Review	**5 min.**	Review for a 20-minute quiz on Lesson 1 for next day.

Additional Activity CD-ROM
DISCOVERING FRENCH INTERACTIVE, (CD-ROM component) Part A, Unit 1, Lesson 1 does an excellent job reviewing and reteaching. **REVIEW**

Homework   Study for Lesson 1 quiz.

© D.C. Heath and Company, a Division of Houghton Mifflin Company

Leçon 2: *Tu es français?*/Leçon 3: *Salut! Ça va?*

DAY 3

TEACHING RESOURCES	TIME	STRATEGIES
1. Warm-up ASSESSMENT OPTIONS Lesson Quiz Portfolio Assessment Test Bank	20 min.	Unit 1, Lesson 1 quiz. Technology: Test Bank Lesson Quiz 1. **PORTFOLIO ASSESSMENT**
2. Listening comprehension: Nationality and numbers ACTIVITY BOOK · CD	15 min.	Do Cassette Worksheets, pp. 7–10 in ACTIVITY BOOK. **MULTIPLE INTELLIGENCES: MUSICAL ❖ CULTURAL AWARENESS**
3. Reading comprehension and cultural awareness ACTIVITY BOOK	15 min.	Do reading and culture activities in ACTIVITY BOOK, pp. 27–28. Have students work in pairs to verify their answers. **CULTURAL AWARENESS ❖ PAIRED/GROUP ACTIVITY**
4. Review: Numbers and nationalities	15 min.	Review numbers (1–20) and adjectives of nationalities. **REVIEW**
5. Greetings STUDENT TEXT	10 min.	Setting the scene for formal or informal greetings, p. T22. Use Overhead Transparency S4. Read the *Note Culturelle* on p. 23 of the textbook. **CULTURAL AWARENESS ❖ MULTIPLE INTELLIGENCES: SPATIAL ❖ PAIRED/GROUP ACTIVITY**
6. Expressions with *ça va?* STUDENT TEXT	15 min.	Present expressions with **ça va?** using Overhead Transparency 5 and pp. 22–23 of the textbook. Model pronunciation for students. **MULTIPLE INTELLIGENCES: SPATIAL**
Homework ACTIVITY BOOK		ACTIVITY BOOK Writing Activities pp. 23–24.

© D.C. Heath and Company, a Division of Houghton Mifflin Company

Leçon 3: *Salut! Ça va?*

DAY 4

TEACHING RESOURCES	TIME	STRATEGIES

1. Warm-up
VIDEODISC **VIDEO BOOK** **CD-ROM**

15 min. Review greetings and expressions of feelings. Play Video Module 3, *Salut! Ça va?* Have students complete Activites 1–3 on pp. 9–10 of the VIDEO ACTIVITY BOOK. **REVIEW ❖ MULTIPLE INTELLIGENCES: SPATIAL**

2. Writing review

10 min. Correct homework.

3. Oral Communication: Asking people how they feel
STUDENT TEXT **VIDEO BOOK**

10 min. Have students pair up and do the *Dialogue* (Activity 2 on p. 24 of the textbook). Then have them do Activity 6 on p. 12 of the VIDEO ACTIVITY BOOK. **PAIRED/GROUP ACTIVITY ❖ PERSONALIZATION**

Additional Activity 👤

A TPR drill to learn how to answer *Ça va?* is *Pour communiquer* on page 17 of TEACHING TO MULTIPLE INTELLIGENCES.

---

4. Numbers
STUDENT TEXT

15 min. Teach numbers 20–60. Do Activity 5 on p. 25 of the textbook. Do TPR activity for numbers and prepositions on p. T25. **TOTAL PHYSICAL RESPONSE**

Additional Activity 1 👤

Use the game *Dix, Vingt, Trente, Quarante* on page 18 of TEACHING TO MULTIPLE INTELLIGENCES to drill the new numbers.

Additional Activity 2 👥

For variety, have students do the dot-to-dot *Qu'est-ce que c'est?* on pp. 2 and 3 of TEACHER TO TEACHER.

---

5. Listening comprehension: Greetings
CD **ACTIVITY BOOK**

15 min. Do Cassette Worksheets, pp. 11–14 in ACTIVITY BOOK. **MULTIPLE INTELLIGENCE: MUSICAL**

© D.C. Heath and Company, a Division of Houghton Mifflin Company

TEACHING RESOURCES	TIME	STRATEGIES
6. Pronunciation: **Les consonnes finales**	10 min.	Play audiocassette, Lesson 3, Section 4. See suggestions on p. T25 of the textbook. MULTIPLE INTELLIGENCE: MUSICAL
7. Review	15 min.	Review for quiz on Lesson 2. COMMUNIPAK: paired and group communication activities on pp. 5–10. REVIEW ❖ MULTIPLE INTELLIGENCE: SPATIAL ❖ PAIRED/GROUP ACTIVITY

Additional Activity 1 COMMUNIPAK
If you have extra time, have students pair up and do the *Tête à Tête* activities on pp. 11–14 of the COMMUNIPAK. PAIRED/GROUP ACTIVITY ❖ PERSONALIZATION ❖ MULTIPLE INTELLIGENCE: SPATIAL

Additional Activity 2
Students may enjoy playing the game *Tour de France* described on pages 15–16 of TEACHING TO MULTIPLE INTELLIGENCES. PAIRED/GROUP ACTIVITY ❖ GAME

© D.C. Heath and Company, a Division of Houghton Mifflin Company

Leçon 3: *Salut! Ça va?*
Leçon 4: *Le français pratique: L'heure*

DAY 5, End of Week 1

TEACHING RESOURCES	TIME	STRATEGIES
1. Warm-up ASSESSMENT OPTIONS Lesson Quiz Portfolio Assessment Test Bank	20 min.	Review for quiz. Lesson 2 quiz. Technology: Test Bank Lesson Quiz 2. **PORTFOLIO ASSESSMENT**
2. Comprehension practice: *L'heure* VIDEODISC CD-ROM	10 min.	Play Video Module 4, *L'heure.* Teach vocabulary for telling time. **MULTIPLE INTELLIGENCE: SPATIAL**
3. Oral Communication: Asking what time it is STUDENT TEXT VIDEO BOOK	15 min.	Do Activities 1 and 2 on p. 13 of the VIDEO ACTIVITY BOOK. Present *Pour communiquer:* how to talk about time, on pp. 26-27 of the textbook. Practice asking and telling time with Activities 1 and 2 on p. 27. Distinction between A.M. and P.M. **PAIRED/GROUP ACTIVITY**
4. Time STUDENT TEXT	15 min.	Teach time with TPR activity using prop: clock with movable hands on p. T27 of the textbook. Introduce quarter hours, half hours and minutes. Include cross-cultural observation on 24-hour clock (T27). **CULTURAL AWARENESS**

Additional Activity 1

Have students explore times in different parts of the world with INTERNET CONNECTION NOTES Project 5 on pp. 10–11. **CULTURAL AWARENESS**

Additional Activity 2

Use the song drill *Quelle heure est-il?* on page 19 of TEACHING TO MULTIPLE INTELLIGENCES to help students learn the time. **TPR** ❖ **MULTIPLE INTELLIGENCE: MUSICAL**

© D.C. Heath and Company, a Division of Houghton Mifflin Company

TEACHING RESOURCES	TIME	STRATEGIES
5. Listening comprehension: What time is it?	15 min.	Play audiocassette or CD, Lesson 4, Sections 1 and 2. Do Activity Book Cassette Worksheet p. 15. Use Overhead Transparency 6, *Quelle heure est-il?* **MULTIPLE INTELLIGENCE: MUSICAL** ❖ **MULTIPLE INTELLIGENCE: SPATIAL**
6. Review	15 min.	Review for quiz on Lesson 3. Have the students do pp. 3 and 4, *Interviews,* in the COMMUNIPAK. Use Transparency 5. **PAIRED/GROUP ACTIVITY** ❖ **CULTURAL AWARENESS** ❖ **REVIEW**

Leçon 4: *Le français pratique: L'heure*

DAY 6

TEACHING RESOURCES	TIME	STRATEGIES
1. Warm-up ASSESSMENT OPTIONS Lesson Quiz · Portfolio Assessment · Test Bank	20 min.	Lesson 3 quiz. Technology: Test Bank Lesson Quiz 3. **PORTFOLIO ASSESSMENT**
2. Oral comprehension: *L'heure*	15 min.	Play Video Module 4. Go over *Mini-scènes* A and B on pp. 26 and 28 of the textbook. Have students complete Activities 3–6 in the VIDEO ACTIVITY BOOK, pp. 14–15. **MULTIPLE INTELLIGENCE: MUSICAL** ❖ **CULTURAL AWARENESS**
3. Oral communication: *L'heure*	15 min.	Practice asking and telling time with Activities 2 and 3 on pp. 27 and 29 of the textbook. Do paired Activities 4 and 5 about time of events on p. 29 and Activity 6, answering questions about train schedules, on p. 29. OR Have students pair up and do *Tête à Tête* 2 on pp. 13 and 14 of the COMMUNIPAK. **PAIRED/GROUP ACTIVITY**
4. Recapitulation and unit review	15 min.	In class, ask students to do *À votre tour,* Activities 1, 2 and 3 on p. 30 of the textbook. **REVIEW** ❖ **PAIRED/GROUP ACTIVITY**

© D.C. Heath and Company, a Division of Houghton Mifflin Company

LEÇON 4, Day 6, *continued*

TEACHING RESOURCES	TIME	STRATEGIES
5. Writing and speaking practice: *Quelle heure est-il?*	15 min.	Play Section 4 of Lesson 4 of the audiocassette or CD. Have students complete the corresponding activity on p. 16 of the ACTIVITY BOOK. **PAIRED/GROUP ACTIVITY** ❖ **MULTIPLE INTELLIGENCE: MUSICAL** **Note:** You can have pairs of students record dialogues based on Activity 4 or 5 on p. 31 of the textbook for an oral portfolio. **PAIRED/GROUP ACTIVITY** ❖ **PORTFOLIO ASSESSMENT**
6. Reading comprehension and cultural awareness: Calling cards and calendars	10 min.	Do Reading and Culture activities in Activity Book pp. 29–30. Review communicative expressions and thematic vocabulary of Activity Book pp.31–32. **CULTURAL AWARENESS** ❖ **REVIEW**
Homework		Study for quiz on Lesson 4.

DAY 7

TEACHING RESOURCES	TIME	STRATEGIES
1. Warm-up ASSESSMENT OPTIONS: Lesson Quiz, Portfolio Assessment, Test Bank	20 min.	Lesson 4 quiz. Technology: Test Bank Lesson Quiz 4. **PORTFOLIO ASSESSMENT**
2. Entracte	15 min.	Have fun doing Entracte 1 on pp. 33–34 with students. Use the teacher suggestions on those pages.
3. Puzzles	20 min.	Have students unscramble words on pp. 1 and 4 of TEACHER TO TEACHER to review the geography of France and phrases for the time.

© D.C. Heath and Company, a Division of Houghton Mifflin Company

TEACHING RESOURCES	TIME	STRATEGIES
4. Unit Review	**35 min.**	Go back and do any Additional Activities you didn't have time for in Days 1–6. Answer any questions students may have about the unit. Review for Unit Test. **REVIEW**

DAY 8

TEACHING RESOURCES	STRATEGIES

ASSESSMENT OPTIONS

■ Portfolio Assessment

PROFICIENCY **TESTS**

- Listening Comprehension Performance Test
- Reading Performance Test
- Speaking Performance Test
- Writing Performance Test
- Unit Test (Achievement)
- Test Bank (Computerized)

CD-ROM Cahier, Exploration

At this point you may choose which testing option you want to use, depending on your teaching style and the needs and make-up of your particular class. For a Unit Test, see the Testing and Assessment Kit. There are many options available in DISCOVERING FRENCH and there is a great deal of flexibility. Depending on your teaching style and the make-up of your classroom, you may wish to use any or all of the tests shown at the left.

Administer Unit Test 1 from the Testing and Assessment Kit. This will probably take some students the entire period. While they are doing the writing part of the test, you may want to call individual students to your desk to administer the Speaking Proficiency Test.

© D.C. Heath and Company, a Division of Houghton Mifflin Company

UNITÉ 3 Bon Appétit! *by Pamela Knapp*
Leçon 9: *Tu as faim?*

DAY 1

ANSWER KEY Answers to Student Text and COMMUNIPAK activities.

TEACHING RESOURCES	TIME	STRATEGIES
1. Warm-up VIDEO BOOK STUDENT TEXT	10 min.	Show Video Module 9 *Dialogue: Tu as faim?* Replay using audiocassette or CD while students follow with textbook p. 58. Have them first listen, then repeat scenes 1 and 2. Have them complete p. 33 of the VIDEO ACTIVITY BOOK to make sure they understood. **MULTIPLE INTELLIGENCE: MUSICAL** ❖ **MULTIPLE INTELLIGENCE: SPATIAL**
2. Oral comprehension: ***Tu as faim?*** ACTIVITY BOOK STUDENT TEXT	10 min.	Introduce vocabulary on p. 59 of the textbook. Have the students repeat the words and phrases after you. Ask them to open their ACTIVITY BOOKS to p. 63 and complete Activity C in Section 2 while they listen to the audiocassette. You can also use Overhead Transparency S8, *Au fast-food.* **MULTIPLE INTELLIGENCE: MUSICAL** ❖ **MULTIPLE INTELLIGENCE: SPATIAL**
3. Vocabulary: *Qu'est-ce que tu veux?*	5 min.	Practice the vocabulary further by asking students questions such as, **«Tu as faim?»** and **«Qu'est-ce que tu veux?»** Students can answer using food items from Overhead Transparency 10, *Les nourritures.* **MULTIPLE INTELLIGENCE: SPATIAL** ❖ **PERSONALIZATION**

Additional Activity 1
Les nourritures   Have fun practicing food vocabulary with the drill *Les nourritures* on p. 43 of TEACHING TO MULTIPLE INTELLIGENCES. **GAME** ❖ **PAIRED/GROUP ACTIVITY** ❖ **PERSONALIZATION**

Additional Activity 2
Les nourritures   Have students do Internet Project 1 on p. 21 of INTERNET CONNECTION NOTES using the Web to find their favorite snacks in Paris! **PERSONALIZATION** ❖ **TECHNOLOGY**

Additional Activity 3
Au restaurant   Have students interview each other using p. 39 of the COMMUNIPAK. They will take each other's orders in a French restaurant!

© D.C. Heath and Company, a Division of Houghton Mifflin Company

TEACHING RESOURCES	TIME	STRATEGIES
4. *Les jeunes et la nourriture* STUDENT TEXT	5 min.	Ask students to read the *Note culturelle* on p. 59. Ask them to compare the way they eat to the way French teenagers eat. **CULTURAL AWARENESS ❖ PERSONALIZATION**
5. Masculine and feminine STUDENT TEXT	5 min.	Briefly present the information in the green grammar box on p. 60 of the textbook. Be sure that students understand the difference between the definite and indefinite article.
6. Choosing foods STUDENT TEXT	5 min.	Call on individual students to do Activities 1 and 2 (p. 60), choosing and asking for certain foods, orally. **PAIRED/GROUP ACTIVITY ❖ PERSONALIZATION**
Homework		Assign p. 73, Writing Activities, in the ACTIVITY BOOK.

© D.C. Heath and Company, a Division of Houghton Mifflin Company

LEÇON 9, *continued*

DAY 2

TEACHING RESOURCES	TIME	STRATEGIES
1. Warm-up	10 min.	Check homework and go over it with the class, calling on individual students to give the correct answers. Ask how many got the *Flash culturel* question right. Ask students to see how many French cheeses they can name. **CULTURAL AWARENESS ❖ REVIEW**
2. Ordering food VIDEODISC	5 min.	Play Video Module 9 *Mini-scènes: Ordering Food.* Call on volunteers to supply the answers to the questions they hear in the *Now it's your turn* segment.
3. *Tu as faim?* STUDENT TEXT	5 min.	Have students do Activity 3 on p. 61 of the textbook orally in pairs. If some pairs do a very good job, arrange to record their scene on video or audiocassette for their portfolio. **PORTFOLIO ASSESSMENT ❖ PAIRED/GROUP ACTIVITY**

Additional Activity VIDEO BOOK
Have students complete Activities 2 and 3, *Tout le monde a faim!* and *Je voudrais* on p. 34 of the VIDEO ACTIVITY BOOK. **PAIRED/GROUP ACTIVITY**

4. *Qu'est-ce que tu veux?* STUDENT TEXT	5 min.	Do Activity 4 on p. 61 of the textbook with the entire class orally, asking for volunteers to supply an appropriate food item. **PERSONALIZATION ❖ PAIRED/GROUP ACTIVITY**
5. *Tu as faim?* CD ACTIVITY BOOK	5 min.	Have students open their ACTIVITY BOOKS to p. 63. Play Section 2, Activity D of the audiocassette or CD as they complete this activity. Play Section 3 as student volunteers give answers orally.
6. *Prononciation: L'intonation* ACTIVITY BOOK CD	5 min.	Ask students to open their ACTIVITY BOOKS to p. 64. Have them do Activity F orally as they listen to the audiocassette or CD.

© D.C. Heath and Company, a Division of Houghton Mifflin Company

TEACHING RESOURCES	TIME	STRATEGIES

Additional Activity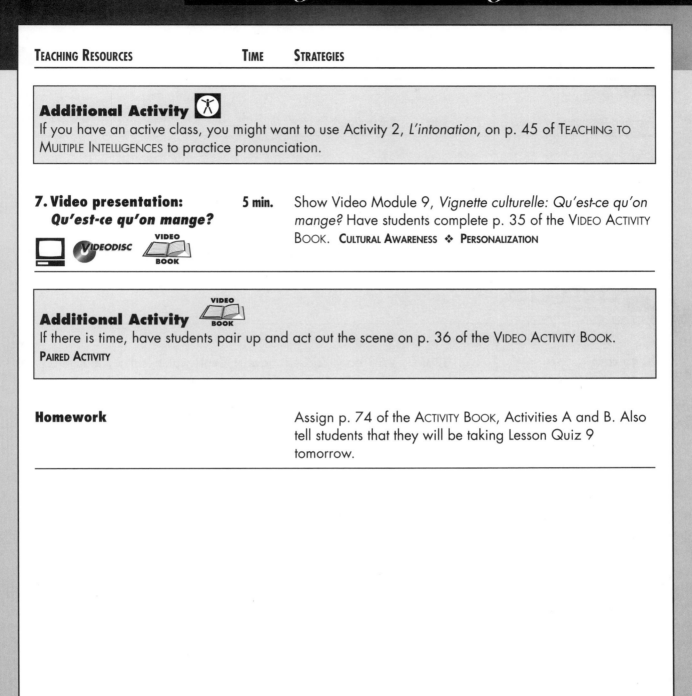

If you have an active class, you might want to use Activity 2, *L'intonation,* on p. 45 of TEACHING TO MULTIPLE INTELLIGENCES to practice pronunciation.

7. Video presentation: 5 min.   Show Video Module 9, *Vignette culturelle: Qu'est-ce qu'on*
Qu'est-ce qu'on mange?   *mange?* Have students complete p. 35 of the VIDEO ACTIVITY
                                     BOOK. **CULTURAL AWARENESS** ❖ **PERSONALIZATION**

Additional Activity

If there is time, have students pair up and act out the scene on p. 36 of the VIDEO ACTIVITY BOOK.
PAIRED ACTIVITY

Homework   Assign p. 74 of the ACTIVITY BOOK, Activities A and B. Also tell students that they will be taking Lesson Quiz 9 tomorrow.

© D.C. Heath and Company, a Division of Houghton Mifflin Company

Leçon 9: *Tu as faim?*/Leçon 10: *Au café*

DAY 3

TEACHING RESOURCES	TIME	STRATEGIES
1. Warm-up	5 min.	Check homework and go over it orally. You may also ask students to write their answers on the board so that any errors can be corrected. **REVIEW**
2. Quiz ASSESSMENT OPTIONS Lesson Quiz Portfolio Assessment Test Bank	15 min.	Administer Lesson Quiz 9. Technology: Test Bank Lesson Quiz 9. **PORTFOLIO ASSESSMENT**
3. *Au café* VIDEODISC ACTIVITY BOOK CD	10 min.	With books closed, have students watch Video Module 10 *Dialogue: Au café.* Then have them open their ACTIVITY BOOKS to p. 65. Play Section 1 of the audiocassette or CD. Students will do Activities A *(Compréhension orale)* and B *(Écoutez et répétez)* as they listen to the tape.

Additional Activity VIDEO BOOK

Have students complete p. 37 of the VIDEO ACTIVITY BOOK.

---

4. Learning to ask for something STUDENT TEXT	10 min.	Ask students to open their textbooks to p. 63. Introduce the vocabulary in the *Pour communiquer* box. Have students repeat the words and expressions, and ask them to tell you (in French) which beverage they prefer from the list. Use Overhead Transparencies S7 and 11. **PERSONALIZATION** ❖ **MULTIPLE INTELLIGENCES: SPATIAL**

Additional Activity 1 COMMUNIPAK

Have students interview other students to find out what they would like to order using the COMMUNIPAK, p. 45.

© D.C. Heath and Company, a Division of Houghton Mifflin Company

Additional Activity 2
For a different kind of drill on *Les boissons,* use pp. 47–48 in TEACHING TO MULTIPLE INTELLIGENCES.
PAIRED/GROUP ACTIVITY

Additional Activity 3
For those using INTERNET CONNECTION NOTES, have students complete Internet Project 2 on p. 22.
TECHNOLOGY

Leçon 10: *Au café*

DAY 4

TEACHING RESOURCES	TIME	STRATEGIES
1. Warm-up	5 min.	Return Lesson Quiz 9 and go over it. REVIEW
2. *Le café* STUDENT TEXT	5 min.	Ask students to read the *Note culturelle* on p. 63 of the textbook and give their reactions to the concept of the French café. Ask them if they have anything similar in their own town or city. CULTURAL AWARENESS ❖ PERSONALIZATION
3. Choosing a beverage STUDENT TEXT	5 min.	Do Activities 1 and 3 on pp. 64 and 65 of the textbook orally with the entire class. Use Overhead Transparencies 10 and 11. PAIRED/GROUP ACTIVITY ❖ PERSONALIZATION
4. In a café STUDENT TEXT	5 min.	Have students do Activities 2 and 4 on pp. 64 and 65 orally in pairs. PAIRED/GROUP ACTIVITY ❖ PERSONALIZATION
5. Saying please VIDEODISC	5 min.	Play Video Module 10 *Mini-scènes: Saying please.* Have student volunteers supply the answers to the questions in the "Now it's your turn" section. CULTURAL AWARENESS

DAY 4 (cont.)

Additional Activity

Have students complete Activity 2, *S'il vous plaît,* on p. 38 of the Video Activity Book.

---

6. *S'il vous plaît ou s'il te plaît?*

10 min.   Have students turn to p. 66 in their Activity Book. As they listen to Sections 2, 3, and 4 of the Lesson 10 audiocassette or CD, they should complete the corresponding Activities C, D, E and F.

---

7. *Prononciation: L'accent final*

5 min.   Continuing with the audiocassette, do Section 5 on p. 68 of the Activity Book.

Homework

Assign the writing activities for Lesson 10 on pp. 75 and 76 in the Activity Book. Also tell students to prepare for Lesson Quiz 10.

Additional Activities

1. Show the *Vignette culturelle: Qu'est-ce qu'on boit?* and let students complete p. 39 of the Video Activity Book.
2. Students might enjoy dramatizing what they have learned using Activity 4, *Vous désirez?* on p. 40 of the Video Activity Book.

© D.C. Heath and Company, a Division of Houghton Mifflin Company

Leçon 11: *Ça fait combien?*

DAY 5

TEACHING RESOURCES	TIME	STRATEGIES
1. Warm-up	**10 min.**	Go over homework. Have student volunteers write the answers to each activity on the board so that any errors can be spotted and corrected. **REVIEW**
2. Quiz **ASSESSMENT OPTIONS** Lesson Quiz Portfolio Assessment Test Bank	**15 min.**	Administer Lesson Quiz 10. Technology: Test Bank Lesson Quiz 10. **PORTFOLIO ASSESSMENT**
3. How much is it? VIDEODISC	**5 min.**	Show Video Module 11 *Dialogue: Ça fait combien?* and *Mini-scènes: Asking what one owes.* **CULTURAL AWARENESS**

Additional Activity VIDEO BOOK
Have students complete Activities 1 and 2 on p. 41 of the VIDEO ACTIVITY BOOK.

| **4. Oral comprehension:**
Ça fait combien?
ACTIVITY BOOK | **10 min.** | Ask students to turn to p. 69 in their ACTIVITY BOOKS. Using the Lesson 11 audiocassette or CD, have students complete listening Activities A, B and C. |

Additional Activity COMMUNIPAK
Have students pair up and complete the *Tête à Tête* Activity 1, *Combien Coûte . . .?* on pp. 47 and 48 of the COMMUNIPAK. **PAIRED/GROUP ACTIVITY**

| **Homework** | | Assign Writing Activity 1, p. 77 of the ACTIVITY BOOK. |

© D.C. Heath and Company, a Division of Houghton Mifflin Company

LEÇON 11, *continued*

DAY 6

TEACHING RESOURCES	TIME	STRATEGIES
1. Warm-up	**5 min.**	Return Lesson Quiz 10 and go over it. **REVIEW**
2. Review	**5 min.**	Check homework and go over it orally with class. You may write the answers on the board as the students read them aloud. **REVIEW**

Additional Activities

For another way of drilling *Ça fait combien?*, do Activity 4 on pp. 49-50 of TEACHING TO MULTIPLE INTELLIGENCES. You can also have students pair up for Activity 5 on p. 51 of MULTIPLE INTELLIGENCES. **PAIRED/GROUP ACTIVITY**

3. French money **VIDEODISC**	**10 min.**	Show Video Module 11, *Vignette culturelle: L'argent français*. Then show students real examples of French coins and bills if possible. Ask them to compare French and American bills. **CULTURAL AWARENESS**

Additional Activity

Have students complete pp. 42-43 of the VIDEO ACTIVITY BOOK. If there is time they can act out the restaurant scene on p. 44. You might want to use Overhead Transparency 12, *Menu from Le Select* here.

4. S'il te plaît **STUDENT TEXT**	**15 min.**	Ask students to open their textbooks to p. 68. Do Activity 1 orally with the entire class. Use Overhead Transparency 12, *Menu from Le Select*. Then ask students to do Activities 2, 3 and 4 orally with a partner. Have the pairs present Activity 4 to the class. **PAIRED/GROUP ACTIVITY** ❖ **CULTURAL AWARENESS**

Additional Activity

Have students do Internet Project 3 on p. 23 of INTERNET CONNECTION NOTES to find what everyday objects cost in France.

© D.C. Heath and Company, a Division of Houghton Mifflin Company

Teaching Resources	Time	Strategies
5. *Au café* and *Prononciation: La consonne 'r'*	5 min.	Using the audiocassette or CD for Lesson 11, have students do Listening Activities D and E on p. 70 in the ACTIVITY BOOK.
Homework		Assign Writing Activity 2 on p. 78 in the ACTIVITY BOOK for tomorrow. Also tell students to prepare for Lesson Quiz 11.

© D.C. Heath and Company, a Division of Houghton Mifflin Company

Leçon 12: *Le français pratique: Le temps*

DAY 7

TEACHING RESOURCES	TIME	STRATEGIES
1. Warm-up	5 min.	Check homework, then have students write the answers on the board. Ask the students who wrote the sentences to read them aloud. Correct any written or oral mistakes. **REVIEW**
2. Quiz **ASSESSMENT OPTIONS** Lesson Quiz Portfolio Assessment Test Bank	15 min.	Administer Lesson Quiz 11. Technology: Test Bank Lesson Quiz 11. **PORTFOLIO ASSESSMENT**
3. *Le temps** ACTIVITY BOOK · CD	5 min.	Ask students to open their ACTIVITY BOOKS to p. 71. Using the audiocassette or CD for Lesson 12, have them do Listening Exercises A and B.
4. *Le temps* VIDEODISC · VIDEO BOOK	5 min.	Play Video Module 12 *Dialogue: Le temps* and have students complete Activity 1 on p. 45 of the VIDEO ACTIVITY BOOK.
5. How to talk about the weather STUDENT TEXT	5 min.	Present the weather expressions in the *Pour communiquer* box on p. 71 of the text.
6. Talking about the weather VIDEODISC	5 min.	Play Video Module 12, *Mini-scènes: Talking about the weather*. Ask for student volunteers to respond to the questions in the *Now it's your turn* activity.

Additional Activity   VIDEO BOOK

Have students complete Activity 2: *La date et le temps,* on p. 45 of the VIDEO ACTIVITY BOOK.

© D.C. Heath and Company, a Division of Houghton Mifflin Company

TEACHING RESOURCES	TIME	STRATEGIES
7. Weather expressions STUDENT TEXT	5 min.	Have students open their textbooks to p. 71. Do Activities 1 and 2 orally with the entire class.

Additional Activity 1
Have students complete Internet Project 4, *Le temps,* to use the Internet to find out what the weather is like today in different parts of the world.

Additional Activity 2
Students may enjoy the word puzzle *Quel temps fait-il?* on p. 6 of TEACHER TO TEACHER. **TECHNOLOGY**

Homework Assign the Writing Activities for Lesson 12 on pp. 79 and 80 in the ACTIVITY BOOK for homework.

---

* **Note:** If your class period is exactly 40 minutes, choose either Activity 3 or Activity 4.

© D.C. Heath and Company, a Division of Houghton Mifflin Company

LEÇON 12, *continued*

DAY 8

Teaching Resources	Time	Strategies
1. Warm-up	**5 min.**	Return Lesson Quiz 11 and go over it. **REVIEW**
2. Seasons and weather	**5 min.**	Check homework, then go over it with the class. **REVIEW**

Additional Activity VIDEO BOOK

Have students practice weather expressions using Activity 5, *Quel temps fait-il?* on p. 48 of the VIDEO ACTIVITY BOOK. **PAIRED/GROUP ACTIVITY ❖ CULTURAL AWARENESS**

---

3. À votre tour! STUDENT TEXT	**10 min.**	Ask students to work with a partner to do Activities 1 through 4 in the *À votre tour* section of Lesson 12 (pp. 72–73 in the textbook). Be sure to walk around the classroom to monitor the students and correct any pronunciation errors. **PAIRED/GROUP ACTIVITY**
4. Drama presentation STUDENT TEXT	**10 min.**	Ask students to get into groups of three. Have each group prepare Activity 5 on p. 73 of the textbook. Ask each group to present their conversation to the class. **PAIRED/GROUP ACTIVITY ❖ CULTURAL AWARENESS ❖ PERSONALIZATION**

Additional Activity COMMUNIPAK

Have students pair up and complete the *Tu as la parole* activities, discussing foods and weather, on pp. 41 and 42 of the COMMUNIPAK.

---

5. La date, la saison et le temps STUDENT TEXT	**5 min.**	Have the class do Activity 6 on p. 73 orally. Use Overhead Transparency 13, *Quel temps fait-il?*

Additional Activity

Students may enjoy the word scramble puzzle, *Quel temps fait-il?* on p. 6 of TEACHER TO TEACHER.

© D.C. Heath and Company, a Division of Houghton Mifflin Company

TEACHING RESOURCES	TIME	STRATEGIES
6. *Quel temps fait-il?* *	**5 min.**	Ask students to open their ACTIVITY BOOKS to p. 71. Using the audiocassette or CD for Lesson 12, have them do Listening Activities C and D.
7. Geography	**5 min.**	Show Video Module 12, *Vignette culturelle: La géographie de la France.* If there is time, have students complete Activity 3 on p. 46 of the VIDEO ACTIVITY BOOK. You may also want to use Overhead Transparency 1, *The map of France.* **CULTURAL AWARENESS**

Additional Activity 1

If you would like to help your students remember the geography of France, have them complete Activity 4 on p. 47 of the VIDEO ACTIVITY BOOK.

Additional Activity 2

Students may enjoy the word scramble puzzle *Aimez-vous la géographie?* on p.1 of TEACHER TO TEACHER.

Homework		Students should prepare for Lesson Quiz 12.

* **Note:** If your class period is exactly 40 minutes, choose either Activity 6 or Activity 7.

© D.C. Heath and Company, a Division of Houghton Mifflin Company

LEÇON 12, *continued*

DAY 9

TEACHING RESOURCES	TIME	STRATEGIES

1. Warm-up

ASSESSMENT OPTIONS
- Lesson Quiz
- Portfolio Assessment
- Test Bank

5 min. — Administer Lesson Quiz 12. Technology: Test Bank Lesson Quiz 12. **PORTFOLIO ASSESSMENT**

2. Parts of the body

STUDENT TEXT

5 min. — Go over pp. 74 and 75 with the students, using *Alouette* to teach them *Les parties du corps.*

3. Reading

STUDENT TEXT

10 min. — Have the students complete the Reading and Culture Activities on pp. 81 to 83 in their textbooks. Go over the activities when they have completed them. **CULTURAL AWARENESS**

4. Paired Activities

COMMUNIPAK

20 min. — If they have not already done these activities, have students turn to p. 39 in their COMMUNIPAK. Working with a partner, they should complete the *Interviews, Tu as la parole,* and *Conversations* Activities on pp. 39 to 44. You may select pairs to present each activity to the rest of the class or simply walk around the class to monitor the students' progress. **PAIRED/GROUP ACTIVITY**

Homework

STUDENT TEXT

Ask students to read pp. 76 through 79 in the *Entracte* section of their textbook and to write out their answers to the *Activités culturelles* on p. 79. They can also complete p. 56 of TEACHING TO MULTIPLE INTELLIGENCES as they consider the differences between French and American schools. **CULTURAL AWARENESS ❖ PERSONALIZATION**

© D.C. Heath and Company, a Division of Houghton Mifflin Company

DAY 10

TEACHING RESOURCES	TIME	STRATEGIES
1. Warm-up	5 min.	Return Lesson Quiz 12 and go over it. **REVIEW**
2. Cultural Information STUDENT TEXT	5 min.	Have students read the *Notes culturelles* on p. 81 and respond orally to the questions in the *Activité culturelle*. **CULTURAL AWARENESS**
3. Paired Activities COMMUNIPAK	30 min.	Working with a partner, students should complete the *Échanges* and *Tête à Tête* activities in their COMMUNIPAK if they have not done so already. Again, you may want to have the pairs present each activity or you may just want to visit each pair to be sure they are all working well. You may also want to collect the students' COMMUNIPAKS and correct any written work they've done. **PAIRED ACTIVITY**
Homework		Students should prepare for Unit Test 3.

© D.C. Heath and Company, a Division of Houghton Mifflin Company

DAY 11

TEACHING RESOURCES

ASSESSMENT OPTIONS

📁 **Portfolio Assessment**

PROFICIENCY TESTS

▶️ **Listening Comprehension Performance Test**

📕 **Reading Performance Test**

🔊 **Speaking Performance Test**

📝 **Writing Performance Test**

▶️ **Unit Test** (Achievement)

💻 **Test Bank** (Computerized)

💿 **CD-ROM** **Cahier, Exploration**

STRATEGIES

At this point you may choose which testing option you want to use, depending on your teaching style and the needs and make-up of your particular class. For a Unit Test, see the Testing and Assessment Kit. There are many options available in DISCOVERING FRENCH and there is a great deal of flexibility. Depending on your teaching style and the make-up of your classroom, you may wish to use any or all of the tests shown at the left.

Administer Unit Test 3 from the Testing and Assessment Kit. This will probably take some students the entire period. While they are doing the writing part of the test, you may want to call individual students to your desk to administer the Speaking Proficiency Test.

© D.C. Heath and Company, a Division of Houghton Mifflin Company

Unité/Leçon_____

Day	Time	Strategies

© D.C. Heath and Company, a Division of Houghton Mifflin Company

UNITÉ 4 Qu'est-ce qu'on fait? *by Dave Miller*
Leçon 13: *Le français pratique: Mes activités*

DAY 1

Ask students to pre-read pages 88–89 on their own the day before formal presentation.

ANSWER KEY Answers to Student Text and COMMUNIPAK activities.

PRESENTATION

A. Introduce vocabulary (pp. 90–91) using Transparencies 14A and 14B, verbs: -er verbs

Student/group response:
1. *Écoutez et regardez*
2. *Écoutez et répétez*
3. *Oui/Non*
4. Either/Or
5. *Qu'est-ce que c'est?*

B. Play Video Module 13, *Mes activités*
1. Students watch (or watch and respond to) "Now it's your turn" as appropriate to class.
2. Use VIDEO ACTIVITY BOOK Activities 1–7 on pp. 49–52 as appropriate to class.

CULTURAL AWARENESS ❖ PAIRED/GROUP ACTIVITY

C. Introduce *Préférences* (pp. 90–91)
1. Teacher models questions/answers.
2. Teacher models questions; students (individuals or class) respond.
3. Cooperative paired activities (Activities 2, 3, 4, p. 92) (Model an example of each activity before students begin.)

PAIRED/GROUP ACTIVITY

Additional Activity 1
Students draw flashcards for verb drill, pp. 57–58 of TEACHING TO MULTIPLE INTELLIGENCES.

Additional Activity 2
Internet Project 1, websites for activities students have never tried and French pop culture, INTERNET CONNECTION NOTES, p. 27. TECHNOLOGY

D. Homework
Assign corresponding ACTIVITY BOOK exercises (Activities 1–2, p. 105).

© D.C. Heath and Company, a Division of Houghton Mifflin Company

DAY 2

BELL QUIZ: (Using Overhead Transparencies 14a and14b)

Label transparency illustrations (A,B,C,D, etc.). Have students identify correct answers by choosing the correct letter as teacher reads 10 activities (verbs) from those pictured on the transparencies.

RE-INTRODUCTION of *Préférences* (pp. 90–91)

A. Play audiocassette or CD, sections 1–3.
Have students complete corresponding sections on pp. 89 and 90 of the ACTIVITY BOOK.

B. Correct Writing Activities (assigned from Day 1)

PRESENTATION

STUDENT TEXT

A. Introduce *Souhaits* (p. 93)
1. *Écoutez et répétez*
2. Use familiar sample situations from *Préférences* (pp. 90–91) in the new context of:
   je veux   je ne veux pas   je voudrais
3. Paired activity (Activities 5–6 p. 93) **PAIRED/GROUP ACTIVITY**
4. Class activity (Activity 7, *Trois souhaits,* p. 93). (Class survey: Whole class or smaller groups. Student secretary records group preferences and reports to class: *"La majorité préfère.."*)
   PAIRED/GROUP ACTIVITY

STUDENT TEXT

B. Introduce *Invitations* (p. 94)
1. *Écoutez et répétez*
2. Paired activity (Activities 8–9 p. 94) **PAIRED/GROUP ACTIVITY**
3. Play audiocassette or CD, sections 4–5. Have students complete corresponding sections on pp. 91 and 92 of the ACTIVITY BOOK, Activity E, *Compréhension orale,* and Activity F *Écoutez et écrivez.*

ACTIVITY BOOK

C. Homework
Assign Writing Activities B/C on p. 106 of the ACTIVITY BOOK.

© D.C. Heath and Company, a Division of Houghton Mifflin Company

LEÇON 13, *continued*

DAY 3

BELL QUIZ: *(Écrivez en français)*

(Possible questions/answers)
COMMENT DIT-ON?. . .
1. I like *(J'aime)*
2. I like to speak French. *(J'aime parler français.)*
3. I don't like to study. *(Je n'aime pas étudier.)*
4. I would like to travel. *(Je voudrais voyager.)*
5. Do you want to have dinner in a restaurant? *(Est-ce que tu veux dîner au restaurant?)* **PERSONALIZATION**

RE-INTRODUCTION

 A. Show Video Module 13 again
Students respond to "Now it's your turn." **CULTURAL AWARENESS**

 B. Concentration game
Use pictures from *Préférences*, pp. 90–91 behind number cards.
GAME ❖ PAIRED/GROUP ACTIVITY

STUDENT TEXT **C. Review *Souhaits* and *Invitations***
Use pictures from the concentration game on pp. 93 and 94. **REVIEW**

Additional Activity 1
Activity 2, *Trois souhaits*, on p. 59 of TEACHING TO MULTIPLE INTELLIGENCES. Verb drill and guessing game. **GAME**

Additional Activity 2
Internet Project 2, p. 30 of INTERNET CONNECTION NOTES, exploring where you would like to go.
TECHNOLOGY

COMMUNIPAK **D. Select paired activity from the COMMUNIPAK: *Tu as la parole*, pp. 57–58.**
PAIRED/GROUP ACTIVITY

 E. Homework
Assign *À votre tour!* p. 95 of the textbook. (You may not wish to assign all activities in this section.)
Activity 2: *Conversation dirigée*
Activity 3: *Expression personnelle*
PAIRED/GROUP ACTIVITY ❖ PERSONALIZATION

© D.C. Heath and Company, a Division of Houghton Mifflin Company

DAY 4

STUDENT TEXT

ASSESSMENT OPTIONS
- Lesson Quiz
- Portfolio Assessment
- Test Bank

A. Correct *Conversation dirigée* (*À votre tour!* p. 95)
Turn in *Expression personnelle* for teacher correction.

B. QUIZ: Leçon 13
Technology: Test Bank Lesson Quiz 13.   **PORTFOLIO ASSESSMENT**

© D.C. Heath and Company, a Division of Houghton Mifflin Company

Leçon 14: *Qui est là?*

DAY 5

PRESENTATION

A. Play Video Module 14, *Où est Jean-Claude?*
1. Students watch or watch and respond to "Now it's your turn" as appropriate to class.
2. Use VIDEO ACTIVITY BOOK Activities 1–5 on pp. 53–56 as appropriate to class.

CULTURAL AWARENESS ❖ PAIRED/GROUP ACTIVITY

B. Present *Note culturelle, Le mercredi après-midi,* (p. 97) as an introduction to dialogue on p. 96.
1. Read dialogue to students as students follow along in textbooks.
2. *Compréhension* activity (p. 96)
3. Play audiocassette or CD 14, Section 1 and do corresponding Cassette Worksheet activity on p. 93 of the ACTIVITY BOOK.
4. Oral comprehension quiz on dialogue (p. T96)

PRESENTATION (Function)

A. Le verbe *être* et *les pronoms sujets* (pp. 98–99) (see T98)

Additional Activity 1 🕴
Activity 3, *Vous êtes à Paris!,* pp. 60–61 of TEACHING MULTIPLE INTELLIGENCES to drill *être*.

Additional Activity 2 👥
Puzzles: *Être* on pp. 7 and 8 of TEACHER TO TEACHER.

B. *Vocabulaire: Où?* (p. 99) Overhead Transparency 15, *Où sont-ils?*

C. Textbook activities 1, 2, 3 and 4 *En France, À Nice, Où sont-ils?* and *Où?* (pp. 99–100).
(May be done first as teacher/class activity and then as student paired activity.) **PAIRED/GROUP ACTIVITY**

© D.C. Heath and Company, a Division of Houghton Mifflin Company

DAY 5 (cont.)

Additional Activity 1
Activity 4, *Où?* p. 62 of TEACHING TO MULTIPLE INTELLIGENCES.

Additional Activity 2
Internet Projects 3 and 4 on pp. 31 and 32 of INTERNET CONNECTION NOTES.

D. Homework
Writing Activities 1–3 on p. 107 of the ACTIVITY BOOK.

DAY 6

BELL QUIZ: *être/ les pronoms sujets*

1. *Je _____ américain. (suis)*
2. *Tu _____ à Paris. (es)*
3. *Il _____ anglais. (est)*
4. *Nous _____ canadiens. (sommes)*
5. *Vous _____ à Genève. (êtes)*
6. *Elles _____ au restaurant. (sont)*

RE-INTRODUCTION

A. *être/ les pronoms sujets/vocabulaire: où?*
Use Overhead Transparency 16, subject pronouns.
1. Play audiocassette or CD 14, Sections 2 and 3 and do corresponding Cassette Worksheet activities on pp. 93–94 of the ACTIVITY BOOK.
2. Correct Writing Activities 1, 2 and 3 (assigned from Day 5).

© D.C. Heath and Company, a Division of Houghton Mifflin Company

LEÇON 14, Day 6, *continued*

PRESENTATION

A. Introduce *Les questions à réponse affirmative ou négative.*
(See pp. T100–101).
1. Play audiocassette or CD 14, Section 4 and do corresponding Cassette Worksheet activity on p. 94 of the ACTIVITY BOOK.
2. Textbook Activity 5 (p. 101): *Nationalités*

B. Introduce *Expressions pour la conversation* p. 101
Textbook Activity 6 (p. 101): Conversation (Teacher/class activity first, then use as a paired student activity). **PAIRED/GROUP ACTIVITY** ❖ **PERSONALIZATION**

C. Introduce *La négation* (p. 102).
Textbook Activities 7 and 8 (p. 102).

D. Introduce *Vocabulaire: Mots utiles* (p. 103).
Textbook Activities 9 and 10 (p. 103).

Additional Activity COMMUNIPAK

Have students pair up for the *Conversations* on pp. 59 and 60 of the COMMUNIPAK.
PAIRED/GROUP ACTIVITY

E. Homework
Writing Activities 4 and 5 on p. 108 of the ACTIVITY BOOK.

© D.C. Heath and Company, a Division of Houghton Mifflin Company

DAY 7

BELL QUIZ: *Comment dit-on?* . . .

1. of course (*bien sûr*)
2. maybe (*peut-être*)
3. with (*avec*)
4. but (*mais*)
5. from (*de*)

RE-INTRODUCTION

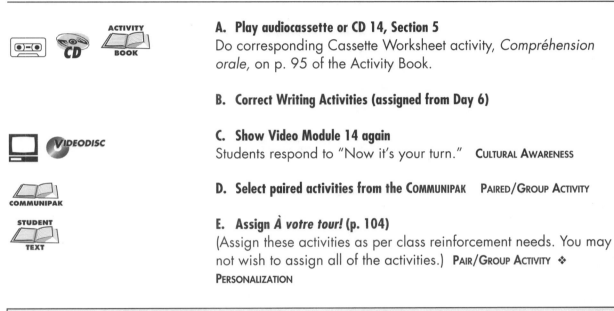

A. Play audiocassette or CD 14, Section 5
Do corresponding Cassette Worksheet activity, *Compréhension orale,* on p. 95 of the Activity Book.

B. Correct Writing Activities (assigned from Day 6)

C. Show Video Module 14 again
Students respond to "Now it's your turn." **CULTURAL AWARENESS**

D. Select paired activities from the COMMUNIPAK **PAIRED/GROUP ACTIVITY**

E. Assign *À votre tour!* (p. 104)
(Assign these activities as per class reinforcement needs. You may not wish to assign all of the activities.) **PAIR/GROUP ACTIVITY** ❖ **PERSONALIZATION**

Additional Activity
Internet Project 3 on p. 31 of INTERNET CONNECTION NOTES.

DAY 8

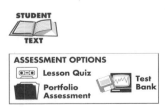

A. Correct *À votre tour!* (p. 104) assigned on Day 7.

B. QUIZ: Leçon 14.
Technology: Test Bank Lesson Quiz 14. **PORTFOLIO ASSESSMENT**

© D.C. Heath and Company, a Division of Houghton Mifflin Company

Block Schedule

Leçon 15: *Une boum*

DAY 9

PRESENTATION

A. Play Video Module 15, *Une boum*
1. Students watch (or watch and respond to) video ("Now it's your turn").
2. Use VIDEO ACTIVITY BOOK Activities on pp. 57–60 as appropriate to class.

B. Present *Note culturelle, Une boum,* (p. 107)
Introduction to Leçon 15 dialogue (see also p. T107).
1. Read dialogue to students as they follow along in textbooks.
2. Do the *Compréhension* (p. 106).

Additional Activity
Project 5, INTERNET CONNECTION NOTES, p. 33. Find an international party on the Internet.

---

3. Play audiocassette or CD 15, Section 1 and do the corresponding Cassette Worksheets on p. 97 of the ACTIVITY BOOK.

PRESENTATION (Function)

A. *Les verbes en -er* (pp. 108–112).
(I prefer to teach this concept all at once. It can be presented in separate parts if desired.)

B. *Vocabulaire: Les verbes en -er*
(Use Overhead Transparencies 14A, 14B, 17)

C. Textbook activities (pp. 108–111).
(See also pp. T108–T111.)
1. *Curiosité*
2. *Quelle activité?*
3. *Le téléscope*
4. *Où sont-ils?* (Oral role-play and paired practice)
5. *Qui?*
6. *À la boum*
7. *Le camp français*
8. *Un voyage à Paris*

© D.C. Heath and Company, a Division of Houghton Mifflin Company

DAY 9 *continued*

Additional Activity

Activity 5, *Quelle activité?* to drill verbs on pp. 63–64 of TEACHING TO MULTIPLE INTELLIGENCES.

DAY 10

BELL QUIZ: *-er* verb vocabulary and conjugation

Fill in the blank with the correct form of any *-er* verb that makes sense.

1. *Je _____ une pizza.* (mange)
2. *Tu _____ la radio.* (écoutes)
3. *Nous _____ français.* (parlons)
4. *Vous _____ en France.* (voyagez)
5. *Ils _____ la télé.* (regardent)

RE-INTRODUCTION

A. Vocabulary concentration game.
Make cue cards using the illustrations from Overhead Transparencies 14A, 14B, 17. **GAME**

B. Play audiocassette or CD 15, Sections 2 and 3.
Do the corresponding Cassette Worksheets on pp. 97-98 of the ACTIVITY BOOK.

PRESENTATION

A. Introduce *Le présent des verbes en -er: forme affirmative et forme négative* (p. 112).
Play audiocassette or CD 15, Section 4, and do the corresponding Cassette Worksheet activity on p. 98 of the ACTIVITY BOOK.

B. Introduce *Vocabulaire: Mots utiles* and *Expressions pour la conversation* (p. 114).
Textbook Activities 12–13 (p. 114).

© D.C. Heath and Company, a Division of Houghton Mifflin Company

LEÇON 15, Day 10, *continued*

Additional Activity 1
Activity 7, a TPR activity on pp. 68–69 of TEACHING TO MULTIPLE INTELLIEGENCES.

Additional Activity 2
Crossword puzzle on p. 9 of TEACHER TO TEACHER.

C. Homework
Writing Activities 1–5 on pp. 109–111 of the ACTIVITY BOOK.

DAY 11

BELL QUIZ

Use Textbook Activity 11: *Un jeu: Weekend!* (p. 113) as a written quiz. Number subjects and illustrations. Students must create complete sentences by combining subject numbers with illustration situations.

RE-INTRODUCTION

A. Correct Writing Activities 1, 2, 3, 4, 5 (assigned from Day 10).

PRESENTATION

A. Introduce *La construction: verbe + infinitif* (p. 115).
1. Textbook activity 14–15 (p. 115)
2. Play audiocassette or CD 15, Section 5, and do the corresponding Cassette Worksheet activity on p. 99 of the ACTIVITY BOOK.

Additional Activity
Project 6, p. 34 of INTERNET CONNECTION NOTES. What do Internet penpals like and dislike doing?

© D.C. Heath and Company, a Division of Houghton Mifflin Company

DAY 11 *continued*

B. Homework
Writing Activity 6: *Communication* on p. 112 of the ACTIVITY BOOK and *À votre tour!* Activities 1, 3, 4 on pp. 116–117 of the textbook. (You may wish to use Activities 2 and 5 as well depending on class needs.)

Additional Activity
Activity 6, Crossword puzzle, on pp. 65–66 of TEACHING TO MULTIPLE INTELLIGENCES to drill verb conjugations and meanings.

DAY 12

A. Correct Writing Activity 6 and *À votre tour!* activities (assigned from Day 11).

B. COMMUNIPAK *Tête à Tête* and *Qu'est-ce que tu aimes faire?* activities on pp. 65–66.   PAIRED/GROUP ACTIVITY

C. QUIZ: Leçon 15
Technology: Test Bank Lesson Quiz 15.   PORTFOLIO ASSESSMENT

ASSESSMENT OPTIONS
Lesson Quiz
Portfolio Assessment
Test Bank

© D.C. Heath and Company, a Division of Houghton Mifflin Company

Leçon 16: *Une interview*

DAY 13

PRESENTATION

A. Play Video Module 16
1. Students watch (or watch and respond to) video "Now it's your turn".
2. Use VIDEO ACTIVITY BOOK Activities on pp. 61 to 63 as appropriate to class.   **CULTURAL AWARENESS**

B. Present *Notes culturelles, Le Sénégal* and *L'Unesco*, (pp. 118–119) as introduction to Leçon 16 dialogue (see also pp. T118–119)
1. Read dialogue to students as they follow along in textbooks.
2. Do the *Compréhension* (p. 119).   **CULTURAL AWARENESS**

Additional Activity

Project 7A, *Sénégal and L'Unesco* on p. 35 of INTERNET CONNECTION NOTES.

---

3. Play audiocassette or CD 16, Section 1 and do the corresponding Cassette Worksheets on p. 101 of the ACTIVITY BOOK.

PRESENTATION (Function)

A. Review *Est-ce que* as an interrogative device.

B. Present *Les questions d'information* (pp. 120–121) *Vocabulaire: Expressions interrogatives* and *Expression pour la conversation* (pp. 120–121).

C. Present *Les expressions interrogatives avec qui* and *Qu'est-ce que?* (pp. 122-123)
Do textbook activities 1–7 (pp. 121–123). (Role-play communication/exchange paired-student activities.)
PAIRED/GROUP ACTIVITY

D. Play audiocassette or CD 16, Sections 2-4.
Do the corresponding Cassette Worksheets on p. 102–103 of the ACTIVITY BOOK.

© D.C. Heath and Company, a Division of Houghton Mifflin Company

DAY 14

BELL QUIZ: Interrogative expressions

Qu'est-ce que ça veut dire? (Écrivez les réponses en anglais.)
1. *Quand?*
2. *Pourquoi?*
3. *Avec qui?*
4. *Comment?*
5. *Qu'est-ce que. . . ?*

RE-INTRODUCTION

COMMUNIPAK

A. COMMUNIPAK
Échanges, Activity 2 (p. 62). *Tête à Tête*, Activity 2 (p. 65) if you have not already done these.   **PAIRED/GROUP ACTIVITY**

Additional Activity
Activity 8, Interrogative Expressions, on pp. 70–71 of TEACHING TO MULTIPLE INTELLIGENCES.

CD   ACTIVITY BOOK

B. Play audiocassette or CD 16, Section 5.
Do the corresponding Cassette Worksheet on p. 103 of the ACTIVITY BOOK.

Additional Activity
Activity 9, Card Game, on pp. 72–74 of TEACHING TO MULTIPLE INTELLIGENCES.   **GAME**

ACTIVITY BOOK

C. Homework
Writing Activities 1–3 on pp. 113–114 of the ACTIVITY BOOK.

PRESENTATION (Function)

STUDENT TEXT

A. *L'interrrogation avec inversion* (p. 125).
(See p. T125.) Textbook Activity 11 (Conversation).

© D.C. Heath and Company, a Division of Houghton Mifflin Company

LEÇON 16, *continued*

DAY 15

BELL QUIZ: Interrogative expressions

Fill in the blank with any interrogative word that makes sense in the context of the sentence.

1. _____ *est-ce que tu es en retard? Parce que ma voiture ne marche pas. (pourquoi)*
2. *Quand* _____ *ton ami organise une boum? Samedi. (est-ce que)*
3. _____ *étudiez-vous? J'étudie avec Paul. (avec qui)*
4. _____ *tu manges? Je mange une pizza. (qu'est-ce que)*
5. _____ *est-ce que tu chantes? Je chante bien! (comment)*

Additional Activity
Project 7B and 7C on p. 36 of INTERNET CONNECTION NOTES. Finding out which countries in Europe use computers most and which radio stations are the most popular. **CULTURAL AWARENESS**

RE-INTRODUCTION

A. Correct Writing Activities (assigned on Day 14).

B. Play Audiocassette or CD 16, Section 5.
Do the corresponding Cassette Worksheet on p. 103 of the ACTIVITY BOOK if you have not already done so.

PRESENTATION

A. Introduce *Le verbe faire* **(p. 124).**
(See p. T124.) *Vocabulaire: Expressions avec faire* (p. 124). Use Overhead Transparency 18.
1. Textbook activities 9 and 10 (p. 124).

Additional Activity ⊠
Activity 10, The verb *faire*, on p. 75 of TEACHING TO MULTIPLE INTELLIGENCES.

© D.C. Heath and Company, a Division of Houghton Mifflin Company

DAY 15 *continued*

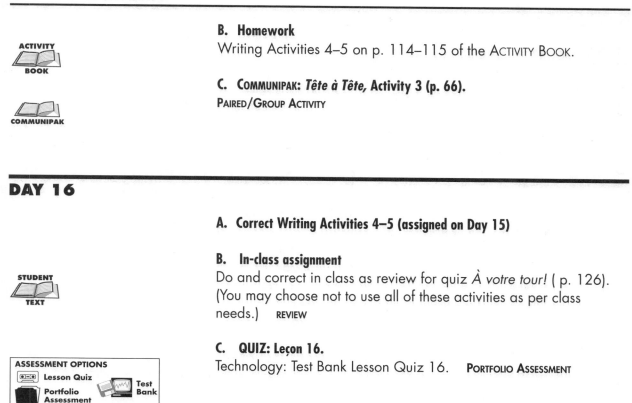

B. Homework
Writing Activities 4–5 on p. 114–115 of the ACTIVITY BOOK.

C. COMMUNIPAK: *Tête à Tête,* **Activity 3 (p. 66).**
PAIRED/GROUP ACTIVITY

DAY 16

A. Correct Writing Activities 4–5 (assigned on Day 15)

B. In-class assignment
Do and correct in class as review for quiz *À votre tour!* (p. 126).
(You may choose not to use all of these activities as per class
needs.)   REVIEW

C. QUIZ: Leçon 16.
Technology: Test Bank Lesson Quiz 16.   PORTFOLIO ASSESSMENT

ASSESSMENT OPTIONS
Lesson Quiz
Portfolio
Assessment
Test Bank

DAY 17

UNITÉ 4: REVIEW

A. Review vocabulary/function in Leçons 13–16
Use individual methodology preferences.   REVIEW
1. Vocabulary list pp. 121–122 of the ACTIVITY BOOK.
2. Reading and culture activities (pp. 117–120).
3. COMMUNIPAK: *Tu as la parole* (pp. 57–58) and *Conversations*
   (pp. 59–60).
CULTURAL AWARENESS ❖ PAIRED/GROUP ACTIVITY ❖ REVIEW

B. Preview the exam   REVIEW

© D.C. Heath and Company, a Division of Houghton Mifflin Company

LEÇON 16, *continued*

DAY 18

EXAMEN: UNITÉ 4

ASSESSMENT OPTIONS

Portfolio
Assessment

PROFICIENCY TESTS

Listening Comprehension
Performance Test

Reading
Performance Test

Speaking
Performance Test

Writing
Performance Test

Unit Test
(Achievement)

Test Bank
(Computerized)

CD-ROM Cahier, Exploration

At this point you may choose which testing option you want to use, depending on your teaching style and the needs and make-up of your particular class. For a Unit Test, see the Testing and Assessment Kit. There are many options available in DISCOVERING FRENCH and there is a great deal of flexibility. Depending on your teaching style and the make-up of your classroom, you may wish to use any or all of the tests shown on the left.

Administer Unit Test 4 from the Testing and Assessment Kit. This will probably take some students the entire period. While they are doing the writing part of the test, you may want to call individual students to your desk to administer the Speaking Proficiency Test.

I use ENTRACTE 4 Activities (pp. 128–133) as out of class QUEST (extra credit) activities for those students who are interested.

© D.C. Heath and Company, a Division of Houghton Mifflin Company

Unité/Leçon_____

Day   **Time**   **Strategies**

_____

_____

_____

_____

_____

_____

_____

_____

_____

_____

_____

_____

_____

_____

_____

_____

_____

_____

_____

_____

_____

_____

_____

_____

© D.C. Heath and Company, a Division of Houghton Mifflin Company

UNITÉ 7 Le shopping by Pamela Knapp
Leçon 25: *Le français pratique: L'achat des vêtements*

DAY 1

TEACHING RESOURCES	**TIME**	**STRATEGIES**

ANSWER KEY Answers to Student Text and COMMUNIPAK activities.

1. Warm-up

STUDENT TEXT

10 min. Have students turn to p. 246 in their textbooks. You may ask them to read the *Accent sur . . . l'élégance française* section silently or aloud. They may have questions about the different types of stores and shops. Ask them to compare typical American shops and flea markets with what exists in France. **CULTURAL AWARENESS ❖ PERSONALIZATION**

2. *Le shopping*

VIDEODISC

5 min. Show Video Module 25 *Introduction* and *Dialogue: Aux Galeries Lafayette.* You can pause the tape at intervals to check students' comprehension. **CULTURAL AWARENESS**

Additional Activity **VIDEO BOOK**

Have students complete Activities 1 and 2 on pp. 103 and 104 of the VIDEO ACTIVITY BOOK.
CULTURAL AWARENESS

---

3. *Qu'est-ce que vous cherchez?*

VIDEODISC **VIDEO BOOK**

5 min. Show Video Module 25: *Mini-scènes: Qu'est-ce que vous cherchez?* This will give the class the opportunity to see and hear the clothing vocabulary you will present next. Have them complete Activity 3 on p. 105 of the VIDEO ACTIVITY BOOK.

Additional Activity

For those using INTERNET CONNECTION NOTES, have students complete Internet Project 1 on p. 75 to find Paris stores on the Web. **TECHNOLOGY**

---

4. Clothing

STUDENT TEXT

10 min. Ask students to open their textbooks to p. 248. Present the vocabulary *(Les vêtements)* and ask students to repeat the words after you. You may also want to have them copy the vocabulary into their notebooks to reinforce the writing skill. Be sure to include the verbs at the top of p. 249. Use Overhead Transparency 35 as a visual aid.

© D.C. Heath and Company, a Division of Houghton Mifflin Company

TEACHING RESOURCES	TIME	STRATEGIES
5. Shopping STUDENT TEXT	**5 min.**	Do Activities 1 and 2 on p. 249 orally with the whole class. **PAIRED/GROUP ACTIVITY** ❖ **CULTURAL AWARENESS** ❖ **PERSONALIZATION**
6. *D'autres vêtements* STUDENT TEXT	**10 min.**	Ask students to turn the page and present the vocabulary *D'autres vêtements et accessoires* to them. Again, you may ask them to copy it into their notebooks as they repeat each word after you. You may find Overhead Transparency 36 helpful here.

Additional Activity 1

Students can have fun finding websites for Paris stores as they investigate sale prices in Paris using Internet Project 2 on p. 76 of INTERNET CONNECTION NOTES. **TECHNOLOGY**

Additional Activity 2 COMMUNIPAK

Cadeaux d'anniversaire Have students pair up for the *Tête à Tête* activity on pp. 134 and 135 of the COMMUNIPAK. They will be guessing what birthday presents their partner is buying for various friends. **PAIRED/GROUP ACTIVITY**

Homework	Assign Writing Activities 1, 2 and 3 on pp. 219–221 in the ACTIVITY BOOK.

© D.C. Heath and Company, a Division of Houghton Mifflin Company

Leçon 25: *Le français pratique: L'achat des vêtements*

DAY 2

TEACHING RESOURCES	TIME	STRATEGIES
1. Warm-up	5 min.	Review vocabulary by showing Video Module 25 *Mini-scènes: Speaking—Vous désirez?* **CULTURAL AWARENESS**

Additional Activity
Have students complete Activity 4 on p. 105 of the VIDEO ACTIVITY BOOK. **CULTURAL AWARENESS**

2. *L'achat des vêtements*	5 min.	To review vocabulary further and practice listening, play audiocassette or CD 25, Sections 1 and 2 while students do Activities A and B on pp. 203–204 in the ACTIVITY BOOK.

Additional Activity
Have your students pair up to practice using their new vocabulary in the *Conversations* on pp. 125 and 126 of the COMMUNIPAK. **PAIRED/GROUP ACTIVITY**

3. Review	10 min.	Go over homework with the class. Ask for volunteers to write their answers on the board. **REVIEW**

4. *Qu'est-ce que tu portes?*	5 min.	Ask students to open their textbooks to p. 250. Do Activities 3 and 4 orally with the whole class. **PAIRED/GROUP ACTIVITY** ❖ **PERSONALIZATION**

Additional Activity
Have students unscramble the words in the two *Traduction, s'il vous plaît* puzzles on pp. 16 and 17 of TEACHER-TO-TEACHER.

© D.C. Heath and Company, a Division of Houghton Mifflin Company

TEACHING RESOURCES	TIME	STRATEGIES

5. Writing practice: *Un jeu*

STUDENT TEXT

5 min.

Have students open their texts to p. 251. Ask them to write out Activity 5. They will have five minutes to create as many sentences as they can. You may ask them to do this individually or in pairs or small groups. You could turn it into a contest with a small prize for the most correct sentences. **GAME** ❖ **PAIRED/GROUP ACTIVITY**

Additional Activity 1

Have students draw clothes for *Les vêtements*, version A or B on pp. 18 and 19 of TEACHER-TO-TEACHER.

Additional Activity 2

Let students draw as they practice the new vocabulary with Activity 1, *Les vêtements,* on p. 109 of TEACHING TO MULTIPLE INTELLIGENCES.

---

6. Shopping and numbers

STUDENT TEXT

15 min.

Present the vocabulary on pp. 252 and 253, *Dans un magasin* and *Les nombres de 100 à 1000,* and ask students to repeat the words and expressions after you. You may want to have students copy the vocabulary into their notebooks. Use Overhead Transparency 37, *Comparing clothing.*

Additional Activity

Have students complete Internet Project 3, shopping in pairs for clothes, on p. 78 of INTERNET CONNECTION NOTES. **PAIRED/GROUP ACTIVITY** ❖ **TECHNOLOGY** ❖ **CULTURAL AWARENESS** ❖ **PERSONALIZATION**

Homework

Assign Writing Activity 4 on p. 222 of the ACTIVITIY BOOK.

© D.C. Heath and Company, a Division of Houghton Mifflin Company

Leçon 25: *Le français pratique: L'achat des vêtements*

DAY 3

TEACHING RESOURCES	TIME	STRATEGIES
1. Warm-up	**5 min.**	Go over homework. **REVIEW**
2. Oral comprehension	**5 min.**	Play the *Mini-scènes: Speaking—Combien coûte la veste?* and *Comment trouves-tu ma robe?* of Video Module 25. Have students complete Activities 5 and 6 on p. 106 of the VIDEO ACTIVITY BOOK. **CULTURAL AWARENESS**
3. Shopping for clothes	**10 min.**	Have students do Cassette Worksheet Activities C, D, E and F (pp. 204–205) in ACTIVITY BOOK.
4. Shopping for clothes	**5 min.**	Ask students to open their textbooks to p. 253. Do Activities 7 and 8 orally with the whole class. **PAIRED/GROUP ACTIVITY** ❖ **PERSONALIZATION**

Additional Activity 1
Let students act out shopping scenes in small groups using Activity 2 *Dans un magasin,* on p. 110 of TEACHING TO MULTIPLE INTELLIGENCES. **PAIRED/GROUP ACTIVITY**

Additional Activity 3
Shopping for a vacation Have students have fun interviewing classmates using *Échanges* 2 on p. 130 of the COMMUNIPAK.

5. À votre tour!	**10 min.**	Have students work with a partner to do Activities 1, 2 and 3 in the *À votre tour* section of their text (pp. 254–255). **PAIRED/GROUP ACTIVITY**

© D.C. Heath and Company, a Division of Houghton Mifflin Company

TEACHING RESOURCES	TIME	STRATEGIES
6. Describing what is wrong with clothing and what you will need on a trip STUDENT TEXT	10 min.	Ask students to write out Activities 4 and 5 on p. 255. You may want to collect these for grading.
Homework		Assign Activity 6 on p. 255 of the textbook. Also tell students to prepare for Lesson Quiz 25.

© D.C. Heath and Company, a Division of Houghton Mifflin Company

Leçon 25: *Le français pratique: L'achat des vêtements*
Leçon 26: *Rien n'est parfait!*

DAY 4

TEACHING RESOURCES	TIME	STRATEGIES
1. Warm-up		Collect homework.
2. Vocabulary review: What people are wearing	10 min.	Quickly review vocabulary from the lesson by asking students personalized questions such as, **«Qu'est-ce que tu portes aujourd'hui?»** etc. Show pictures from magazines and ask students to describe the clothing and give the approximate prices of the items. You can also use Overhead Transparencies 35, 36 and 38. REVIEW ❖ PAIRED/GROUP ACTIVITY ❖ PERSONALIZATION
3. Where to buy clothes	5 min.	Show the *Vignette culturelle* segment of Video Module 25. CULTURAL AWARENESS

Additional Activities
1. Have students complete Activity 7 on p. 107 of the VIDEO ACTIVITY BOOK. CULTURAL AWARENESS
2. Activity 8 on p. 108 gives pairs of students an opportunity to create dialogues based on shopping. PAIRED/GROUP ACTIVITY

4. Quiz ASSESSMENT OPTIONS: Lesson Quiz, Portfolio Assessment, Test Bank	20 min.	Administer Lesson Quiz 25. Technology: Test Bank Lesson Quiz 25. PORTFOLIO ASSESSMENT
5. Deciding what to buy	10 min.	Show Video Module 26 *Dialogue: Rien n'est parfait!* Students may follow along in their textbook (pp. 256–257). Have students complete Activities 1 and 2 on p. 109 of the VIDEO ACTIVITY BOOK. CULTURAL AWARENESS

© D.C. Heath and Company, a Division of Houghton Mifflin Company

TEACHING RESOURCES	TIME	STRATEGIES

Additional Activity
Have students complete Internet Project 4 on p. 79 of INTERNET CONNECTION NOTES.   **TECHNOLOGY**

Homework		Assign the *Compréhension* questions on p. 257 of the textbook in writing.

Leçon 26: *Rien n'est parfait!*

DAY 5

TEACHING RESOURCES	TIME	STRATEGIES
1. Warm-up		Collect homework.
2. Review	10 min.	Return Lesson Quiz 25 and go over it. **REVIEW**
3. Verbs: *Acheter and préférer* STUDENT TEXT	10 min.	Present the verbs *acheter* and *préférer* (p. 258 of textbook). Be sure that students copy these into their notebooks, paying close attention to the accent changes. Practice the pronunciation of these verbs by having students repeat the forms several times.

Additional Activity   COMMUNIPAK
Students can enjoy taking surveys and getting advice on shopping using the *Interviews* on pp. 121 and 122 of the COMMUNIPAK.   **PAIRED/GROUP ACTIVITY ❖ PERSONALIZATION**

4. *Achats* STUDENT TEXT	5 min.	Do Activity 1, p. 258, orally with the whole class. **PAIRED/GROUP ACTIVITY**

© D.C. Heath and Company, a Division of Houghton Mifflin Company

TEACHING RESOURCES	TIME	STRATEGIES
5. Verbs like *acheter* and *préférer* STUDENT TEXT	**5 min.**	Present the verbs like *acheter* and *préférer* on p. 259 of the textbook. Ask for volunteers to write the forms of some of these verbs on the board.
6. *Amener* and *apporter* STUDENT TEXT	**10 min.**	Ask students to write out Activity 2 on p. 259 of the textbook. Have volunteers write their sentences on the board and then read them in turn.
7. What I like or hope to do STUDENT TEXT	**5 min.**	Do Activity 3 on p. 259 of the textbook orally with the whole class. **PAIRED/GROUP ACTIVITY** ❖ **PERSONALIZATION**
Homework		Assign Writing Activities 1 and 2 on p. 223 in the ACTIVITY BOOK.

© D.C. Heath and Company, a Division of Houghton Mifflin Company

Leçon 26: *Rien n'est parfait!*

DAY 6

TEACHING RESOURCES	TIME	STRATEGIES
1. Warm-up	10 min.	Have volunteers write the homework on the board. Correct any mistakes in accents. REVIEW
2. Listening comprehension: Clothing preferences	5 min.	Play the *Mini-scènes: Listening—Comment trouves-tu ce pull?* of Video Module 26 and have students complete Activity 3 on p. 110 of the VIDEO ACTIVITY BOOK. CULTURAL AWARENESS
3. Demonstrative adjectives	5 min.	Have students open their textbooks to p. 260. Introduce the demonstrative adjectives, giving examples of each.
4. Role-play: Liking clothes at a store	5 min.	Do Activity 4 on p. 260 of the textbook orally with the entire class. PAIRED/GROUP ACTIVITY
5. Differences of opinion	5 min.	Have students do Activity 5 on p. 260 of the textbook with a partner. You can call on different pairs to present each one to the class. PAIRED/GROUP ACTIVITY
6. Demonstrative adjectives	5 min.	Have students complete Cassette Worksheet Activities C and D on p. 208 in the ACTIVITY BOOK.

Additional Activity 👤
Use Activity 3, *L'adjectif démonstratif*, on p. 111 of TEACHING TO MULTIPLE INTELLIGENCES to drill using a game format.   GAME

© D.C. Heath and Company, a Division of Houghton Mifflin Company

TEACHING RESOURCES	TIME	STRATEGIES
7. Quel café?	5 min.	Play the *Mini-scènes: Listening—Quel café?* segment of Video Module 26 and have students complete Activity 4 on p. 110 of the VIDEO ACTIVITY BOOK. **CULTURAL AWARENESS**
8. Interrogative adjective quel?	5 min.	Ask students to turn to p. 261 in their textbooks. Introduce the four forms of the interrogative adjective *quel*. Using familiar vocabulary, write examples on the board.
Homework		Assign Writing Activities 3 and 4 in the ACTIVITY BOOK, pp. 224–225.

Leçon 26: *Rien n'est parfait!*

DAY 7

TEACHING RESOURCES	TIME	STRATEGIES
1. Warm-up	5 min.	Go over the homework after student volunteers have written their answers on the board. **REVIEW ❖ PAIRED/GROUP ACTIVITY**
2. Quelle veste désirez-vous?	5 min.	Show the *Mini-scènes: Speaking—Quelle veste désirez-vous?* segment of Video Module 26 and have students complete Activity 5 on p. 111 of the VIDEO ACTIVITY BOOK.
3. Preferences	5 min.	Have students do Cassette Worksheet Activity E on p. 209 of the ACTIVITY BOOK.
4. Colors of summer clothing	5 min.	Ask students to open their textbooks to p. 261. Have them do Activity 6 with a partner. **PAIRED/GROUP ACTIVITY**

© D.C. Heath and Company, a Division of Houghton Mifflin Company

TEACHING RESOURCES	TIME	STRATEGIES
5. Personal preferences STUDENT TEXT	5 min.	Do Activity 7 on p. 261 of the textbook orally with the whole class. **PAIRED/GROUP ACTIVITY ❖ PERSONALIZATION**
6. *Mettre* STUDENT TEXT	5 min.	Present the forms of the verb *mettre* on p. 262 of the textbook. As students copy the verb into their notebooks, ask them to repeat the forms several times.

Additional Activity 1 COMMUNIPAK
Have students pair up and ask each other questions in *Tu as la parole* on pp. 123 and 124 of the COMMUNIPAK. **PAIRED/GROUP ACTIVITY ❖ PERSONALIZATION**

Additional Activity 2
Use an acting activity to drill the verb *mettre*, using Activity 4 on p. 112 of TEACHING TO MULTIPLE INTELLIGENCES.

7. Where things go STUDENT TEXT	5 min.	Do Activity 8 on p. 262 of the textbook orally with the whole class OR ask students to create as many sentences as they can in writing in five minutes. Have volunteers read their sentences aloud. **PAIRED/GROUP ACTIVITY**
8. Personal preferences STUDENT TEXT	5 min.	Do Activity 9, *Questions personnelles*, on p. 263 of the textbook orally with the whole class. **PAIRED/GROUP ACTIVITY ❖ PERSONALIZATION**
9. Pronunciation: *Les lettres "e" et "è"* CD ACTIVITY BOOK	5 min.	Do Cassette Worksheet Activity F on p. 210 of the ACTIVITY BOOK.

Additional Activity
Have students complete Internet Project 5 on p. 80 of INTERNET CONNECTION NOTES to compare and express preferences for items pictured. **PERSONALIZATION ❖ CULTURAL AWARENESS ❖ TECHNOLOGY**

© D.C. Heath and Company, a Division of Houghton Mifflin Company

TEACHING RESOURCES	TIME	STRATEGIES
Homework		Assign Writing Activities 5 and 7 (pp. 225–226) in the ACTIVITY BOOK. Also tell students to prepare for Lesson Quiz 26.

Leçon 26: *Rien n'est parfait!*
Leçon 27: *Un choix difficile*

DAY 8

TEACHING RESOURCES	TIME	STRATEGIES
1. Warm-up		Collect homework.
2. Creating dialogues STUDENT TEXT	10 min.	Have students work in pairs to do Activities 1, 2 and 3 in the *À votre tour* section of their textbook (pp. 264–265). You may want to have different pairs present the activities to the class after they've finished. **PAIRED/GROUP ACTIVITY**

Additional Activity

Have students complete Internet Project 6 on p. 81 of INTERNET CONNECTION NOTES, comparing buying things in a store with on the Internet. **TECHNOLOGY**

TEACHING RESOURCES	TIME	STRATEGIES
3. *Un grand magasin* VIDEODISC · VIDEO BOOK	5 min.	Show the *Vignette culturelle* segment of Video Module 26 and have students complete Activity 6 on p. 111 of the VIDEO ACTIVITY BOOK. **CULTURAL AWARENESS**

Additional Activity

Have students play the *Bon Marché* game on p. 112 of the VIDEO ACTIVITY BOOK. **GAME** ❖ **PAIRED/GROUP ACTIVITY** ❖ **CULTURAL AWARENESS**

© D.C. Heath and Company, a Division of Houghton Mifflin Company

TEACHING RESOURCES	TIME	STRATEGIES
4. Quiz **ASSESSMENT OPTIONS** ☐ Lesson Quiz ☐ Portfolio Assessment ☐ Test Bank	**20 min.**	Administer Lesson Quiz 26. Technology: Test Bank Lesson Quiz 26. **PORTFOLIO ASSESSMENT**
5. *Un choix difficile* ▢ **VIDEODISC** **STUDENT TEXT**	**10 min.**	Show Video Module 27 *Dialogue: Un choix difficile.* Students should keep their books closed as they try to understand the general idea. Then show the *Dialogue* section a second time as students follow along in their textbooks, pp 266–267. At the conclusion of the second viewing, ask students to answer orally the *Compréhension* questions on p. 267.

Additional Activity **VIDEO BOOK**

Have students complete Activities 1 and 2 on p. 113 of the VIDEO ACTIVITY BOOK. **CULTURAL AWARENESS**

Homework   Have students write out their answers to the *Compréhension* questions for homework.

© D.C. Heath and Company, a Division of Houghton Mifflin Company

Leçon 27: *Un choix difficile*

DAY 9

TEACHING RESOURCES	TIME	STRATEGIES
1. Warm-up	**10 min.**	Return Lesson Quiz 26 and go over it. Collect homework. **REVIEW**
2. *Finir* STUDENT TEXT	**5 min.**	Ask students to turn to p. 268 in their textbooks and copy the forms of the verb *finir* into their notebooks. Have them repeat the forms several times.
3. The Paris marathon STUDENT TEXT	**5 min.**	Do Activity 1 on p. 268 orally with the whole class. **PAIRED/GROUP ACTIVITY**
4. Regular *-ir* verbs STUDENT TEXT	**10 min.**	Introduce the other *-ir* verbs like *finir* on p. 268 of the textbook. Ask volunteers to give the forms of these new verbs, both orally and by writing them on the board. Use Overhead Transparency 39 for fun examples of these verbs.
5. Gaining and losing weight STUDENT TEXT	**5 min.**	Do Activity 2 on p. 268 of the textbook orally with the whole class. **PAIRED/GROUP ACTIVITY**
6. Personal questions STUDENT TEXT	**10 min.**	Have students write out the answers to Activity 3, *Questions personnelles,* on p. 269. You can collect these or have students share their answers orally with the class when they've finished. **PAIRED/GROUP ACTIVITY ❖ PERSONALIZATION**
Homework		Assign Writing Activities 1 and 2 on p. 227 in the ACTIVITY BOOK.

© D.C. Heath and Company, a Division of Houghton Mifflin Company

Leçon 27: *Un choix difficile*

DAY 10

TEACHING RESOURCES	TIME	STRATEGIES
1. Warm-up	**5 min.**	Go over homework. REVIEW
2. *Beau, nouveau* and *vieux* STUDENT TEXT	**10 min.**	Ask students to open their textbooks to p. 269 and copy the forms of the adjectives *beau, nouveau* and *vieux* into their notebooks. Practice these by giving the students familiar nouns and asking them to supply the right form of the adjectives for each. Use Overhead Transparency 40.
3. Spring fashions (forms of *beau*) STUDENT TEXT	**5 min.**	Do Activity 4 on p. 269 of the textbook orally with the whole class. PAIRED/GROUP ACTIVITY
4. Differences of opinion STUDENT TEXT	**5 min.**	Have students do Activity 5 orally with a partner. PAIRED/GROUP ACTIVITY
5. Descriptions ACTIVITY BOOK	**5 min.**	Have students do Writing Activity 3 on p. 228 of the ACTIVITY BOOK.
6. Comparisons VIDEODISC VIDEO BOOK	**5 min.**	Play the *Mini-scènes: Listening—Comparisons* segment of Video Module 27 and have students complete Activity 3 on p. 114 of the VIDEO ACTIVITY BOOK. CULTURAL AWARENESS
7. Comparison STUDENT TEXT	**10 min.**	Have students turn to p. 270 in their textbooks and read *La comparaison avec les adjectifs* section. While they are doing this, go to the board and write sentences using the comparative structure with vocabulary the students are familiar with. Be sure to use the adjective *meilleur(e)* also. After the class has finished reading, ask volunteers to read aloud the sentences from the board and tell what they mean in English.

© D.C. Heath and Company, a Division of Houghton Mifflin Company

TEACHING RESOURCES	TIME	STRATEGIES

Additional Activity
Have students complete Internet Project 8 on p. 83 of INTERNET CONNECTION NOTES to give their opinions and find the most popular radio station in Paris.   **TECHNOLOGY** ❖ **PERSONALIZATION**

Homework   Assign Activity 6 on p. 270 of the textbook for homework.

Leçon 27: *Un choix difficile*

DAY 11

TEACHING RESOURCES	TIME	STRATEGIES
1. Warm-up	**5 min.**	Go over the homework. **REVIEW**
2. Comparisons ACTIVITY BOOK CD	**5 min.**	Have students complete Cassette Worksheet Activities C and D on pp. 212–213 of the ACTIVITY BOOK.

Additional Activity
Use Overhead Transparency 37 to practice comparisons with your students.

3. Comparisons VIDEODISC VIDEO BOOK	**5 min.**	Show the *Mini-scènes: Speaking—Comparaisons* segment of Video Module 27 and have students complete Activity 4 on p. 114 of the VIDEO ACTIVITY BOOK. **CULTURAL AWARENESS**

Additional Activity
Students may enjoy breaking a secret code as they practice their comparisons on p. 21 of TEACHER-TO-TEACHER.

4. Personal expression STUDENT TEXT	**5 min.**	Ask students to open their textbooks to p. 271. Have them do Activity 7 orally with a partner. **PAIRED/GROUP ACTIVITY** ❖ **PERSONALIZATION**

© D.C. Heath and Company, a Division of Houghton Mifflin Company

TEACHING RESOURCES	TIME	STRATEGIES
5. Stress pronouns STUDENT TEXT	**5 min.**	Do Activity 8 on p. 271 orally with the whole class. **PAIRED/GROUP ACTIVITY**
6. Prononciation: *Les lettres "ill"* ACTIVITY BOOK CD	**5 min.**	Have students complete Cassette Worksheet Activity E on p. 214 of the ACTIVITY BOOK.
7. À votre tour! STUDENT TEXT	**10 min.**	Working in pairs, have students do Activities 1, 2, and 3 in the *À votre tour* section of their textbooks (pp. 272–273). **PAIRED/GROUP ACTIVITY PERSONALIZATION**
8. Writing proficiency: Describing people STUDENT TEXT	**5 min.**	Have students choose Activity 4 or 5 on p. 273 and write a short composition. Collect it as they finish. **PORTFOLIO ASSESSMENT**
Homework		Assign Writing Activities 4, 5 and 6 on pp. 228 through 230 in the ACTIVITY BOOK. Also tell students to prepare for Lesson Quiz 27.

© D.C. Heath and Company, a Division of Houghton Mifflin Company

Leçon 27: *Un choix difficile*
Leçon 28: *Alice a un job*

DAY 12

TEACHING RESOURCES	TIME	STRATEGIES
1. Warm-up	10 min.	Go over homework by having students write their answers on the board. **REVIEW**
2. At a shopping center	5 min.	Show Video Module 27, *Vignette culturelle: Dans un centre commercial* and have students complete Activity 5 on p. 115 of the VIDEO ACTIVITY BOOK. **CULTURAL AWARENESS**

Additional Activity
Let students have fun role-playing the fashion designer and buyer on p. 116 of the VIDEO ACTIVITY BOOK.

3. Quiz	20 min.	Administer Lesson Quiz 27. Technology: Test Bank Lesson Quiz 12. **PORTFOLIO ASSESSMENT**

ASSESSMENT OPTIONS
Lesson Quiz
Portfolio Assessment
Test Bank

4. A new job	5 min.	Show Video Module 28 *Dialogue: Alice a un job*. Students should not open their textbooks. Then have students open their texts and listen to the dialogue as it is read on Cassette 28. Have students answer the *Compréhension* questions on p. 275 of the textbook orally after they listen to the tape. **CULTURAL AWARENESS**

Additional Activity 1
Have students complete Activities 1 and 2 on p. 117 of the VIDEO ACTIVITY BOOK. **CULTURAL AWARENESS**

Additional Activity 2
Have students complete Internet Project 9 on p. 84 of INTERNET CONNECTION NOTES to find job and internship possibilities through the Internet. **TECHNOLOGY**

© D.C. Heath and Company, a Division of Houghton Mifflin Company

TEACHING RESOURCES	TIME	STRATEGIES
Homework		Have students read the *Note culturelle* on p. 275 of the textbook and write a short comparison (in English) of jobs for young people in France and in the United States. If you are planning to do the *Échanges* activity in the COMMUNIPAK tomorrow, ask students to bring newspaper ads for clothing or bikes, TVs, cameras, etc. They will need to cut off the price. **CULTURAL AWARENESS ❖ PERSONALIZATION**

Leçon 28: *Alice a un job*

DAY 13

TEACHING RESOURCES	TIME	STRATEGIES
1. Warm-up	**10 min.**	Go over Lesson Quiz 27. **REVIEW**
2. Review	**5 min.**	Collect the homework *or* ask volunteers to read their short compositions. **REVIEW**
3. *L'argent* STUDENT TEXT	**10 min.**	Ask students to open their textbooks to p. 276 and follow along as you present the new vocabulary: *l'argent*. Be sure they are comfortable with the spelling change for -*yer* verbs. Ask personalized questions using this vocabulary. (**«Combien de frères as-tu?» «As-tu besoin d'argent?»** etc.) **PAIRED/GROUP ACTIVITY ❖ PERSONALIZATION**
4. Questions and answers STUDENT TEXT	**10 min.**	Have students do Activities 1 and 2 on pp. 276–277 of the textbook, orally with a partner. **PAIRED/GROUP ACTIVITY**

> **Additional Activity**
> Give students an opportunity to express their views regarding money and to see how the French do their banking using Internet Project 10 on p. 85 of INTERNET CONNECTION NOTES. **PERSONALIZATION ❖ TECHNOLOGY**

© D.C. Heath and Company, a Division of Houghton Mifflin Company

TEACHING RESOURCES	TIME	STRATEGIES

5. Speaking proficiency: Saying what you feel like buying; saying what things cost

STUDENT TEXT

| | 5 min. | Do Activities 3 and 4 on p. 277 of the textbook, orally with the whole class.   **PAIRED/GROUP ACTIVITY** ❖ **PERSONALIZATION** |

Additional Activities   COMMUNIPAK

1. Have students pair up to practice finding out how much things cost using *Tête à Tête 1* on pp. 132 and 133 of the COMMUNIPAK.   **PAIRED/GROUP ACTIVITY**
2. Have students do the *Échanges* activity on p. 129 of the COMMUNIPAK. They will be interviewing classmates in French to see if they can guess how much certain items cost.   **PAIRED/GROUP ACTIVITY**

---

6. *Besoin ou envie?*

ACTIVITY BOOK   CD

| | 5 min. | Have students complete Cassette Worksheet Activity B, p. 215 of the ACTIVITY BOOK. |

Leçon 28: *Alice a un job*

DAY 14

TEACHING RESOURCES	TIME	STRATEGIES

1. Warm-up

| | 5 min. | Introduce the pronoun *on* on p. 278 in the textbook. Do Activity 5 orally with the whole class.   **PAIRED/GROUP ACTIVITY** |

Additional Activity

Let students find what languages are spoken in different countries using the websites described in Internet Project 11 on p. 86 of INTERNET CONNECTION NOTES.   **TECHNOLOGY** ❖ **CULTURAL AWARENESS**

---

2. Weekend plans

STUDENT TEXT

| | 5 min. | Have students do Activities 6 and 7 on p. 279 of the textbook orally with a partner.   **PAIRED/GROUP ACTIVITY** ❖ **PERSONALIZATION** |

© D.C. Heath and Company, a Division of Houghton Mifflin Company

TEACHING RESOURCES	TIME	STRATEGIES
3. *Vendre* STUDENT TEXT	10 min.	Present the verb *vendre* on p. 280 of the textbook. When students are comfortable with the forms, have them copy the other *-er* verbs into their notebooks. Call on volunteers to conjugate these verbs on the board. Use Overhead Transparency 41.
4. *Attendre, qui, qu'est-ce qu'ils font?* STUDENT TEXT	10 min.	Do Activities 9, 10 and 11 on pp. 280 and 281 orally with the whole class.
5. *Qu'est-ce qu'on vend ici?* ACTIVITY BOOK CD	5 min.	Have students complete Cassette Worksheet Activity D, p. 216 in the ACTIVITY BOOK.
6. Use of *on* VIDEODISC VIDEO BOOK	5 min.	Play *Mini-scènes: Qu'est-ce qu'on vend?* and *Qu'est-ce qu'on vend ici?* segments of Video Module 28. Have students complete Activities 3 and 4 on p. 118 of the VIDEO ACTIVITY BOOK. **CULTURAL AWARENESS**

Additional Activity VIDEO BOOK

Have students pair up and do Activity 8 on p. 122 of the VIDEO ACTIVITY BOOK. They will be interviewing each other about their new jobs. **PAIRED/GROUP ACTIVITY**

Homework

Assign Writing Activities 1, 2 and 3 on pp. 231 and 232 of the ACTIVITY BOOK.

© D.C. Heath and Company, a Division of Houghton Mifflin Company

Leçon 28: *Alice a un job*

DAY 15

TEACHING RESOURCES	TIME	STRATEGIES
1. Warm-up	**5 min.**	Go over homework. **REVIEW**
2. Use of *on* VIDEODISC VIDEO BOOK	**5 min.**	Play *Mini-scènes: Listening—On dîne?* segment of Video Module 28. After the first viewing, ask students if they have an idea of what *allons* or *dansons* mean. Replay the segment and have students complete Activity 5 on p. 119 of the VIDEO ACTIVITY BOOK.
3. The imperative STUDENT TEXT	**10 min.**	Have students open their textbooks to p. 281. Introduce the forms of the imperative to them.
4. Giving advice STUDENT TEXT	**10 min.**	Do Activities 12, 13 and 14 on p. 282 of the textbook orally with the whole class. **PAIRED/GROUP ACTIVITY**
5. Contradicting your friend STUDENT TEXT	**5 min.**	Have students work with a partner to do Activity 15 on p. 283 of the textbook. **PAIRED/GROUP ACTIVITY**
6. Accepting invitations VIDEODISC VIDEO BOOK	**5 min.**	Play the *Mini-scènes: Speaking—On joue au tennis?* segment of Video Module 28. Have students complete Activity 6 on p. 120 of the VIDEO ACTIVITY BOOK. **CULTURAL AWARENESS**

Additional Activity
Have students explore the classified sections of French newspapers to find out what people are looking for in Internet Project 12 on p. 87 of INTERNET CONNECTION NOTES. **TECHNOLOGY**

© D.C. Heath and Company, a Division of Houghton Mifflin Company

TEACHING RESOURCES	TIME	STRATEGIES
7. What people are doing; accepting invitations	5 min.	Have students complete Cassette Worksheet Activities E and F on p. 217 of their ACTIVITY BOOKS.
Homework		Assign Writing Activities 4, 5 and 6 on pp. 232–233 of the ACTIVITY BOOK. **PERSONALIZATION**

Leçon 28: *Alice a un job*

DAY 16

TEACHING RESOURCES	TIME	STRATEGIES
1. Warm-up	10 min.	Go over homework. **REVIEW**
2. Prononciation: *Les lettres "an" et "en"*	5 min.	Do Cassette Worksheet Activity H on p. 218 of the ACTIVITY BOOK.
3. *À votre tour!*	20 min.	Have students work with a partner to do Activities 1, 2, 3 and 4 in the *À votre tour* section of the textbook, pp. 284–285. You may want to suggest that they change partners after the first two activities. **PAIRED/GROUP ACTIVITY**
Homework		Assign Writing Activity 7 on p. 234 in the ACTIVITY BOOK. Also have students prepare for Lesson Quiz 28. **PERSONALIZATION**

© D.C. Heath and Company, a Division of Houghton Mifflin Company

Leçon 28: *Alice a un job*

DAY 17

TEACHING RESOURCES	TIME	STRATEGIES
1. Warm-up	**10 min.**	Go over homework and answer any questions students may have before the quiz. **REVIEW**
2. Quiz **ASSESSMENT OPTIONS** Lesson Quiz Portfolio Assessment Test Bank	**20 min.**	Administer Lesson Quiz 28. Technology: Test Bank Lesson Quiz 12.
3. *Petit test culturel* STUDENT TEXT	**10 min.**	Have students open their textbooks to p. 286. Do the *Petit test culturel* orally with the entire class. **CULTURAL AWARENESS**

> **Additional Activity**
>
> Let students find out more about *Les 3 Suisses* in Internet Project 13 on p. 88 of INTERNET CONNECTION NOTES. **CULTURAL AWARENESS ❖ TECHNOLOGY**

4. *Variétés* STUDENT TEXT	**5 min.**	Do the *Variétés* activity on p. 290 of the textbook orally with the entire class. **PERSONALIZATION ❖ PAIRED/GROUP ACTIVITY**
Homework		Assign the *Entre amis* reading and activity on pp. 288–289 of the textbook.

© D.C. Heath and Company, a Division of Houghton Mifflin Company

Leçon 28: *Alice a un job*

DAY 18

TEACHING RESOURCES	TIME	STRATEGIES
1. Warm-up	**10 min.**	Return Lesson Quiz 28 and go over it. REVIEW
2. Review	**5 min.**	Go over the homework. REVIEW
3. Boutiques and sales ACTIVITY BOOK	**20 min.**	Have students do Activities A and B on pp. 235–237 in the ACTIVITY BOOK. Go over the answers when all have finished. CULTURAL AWARENESS
4. Interviews COMMUNIPAK	**10 min.**	Have students work with a partner to complete the *Interviews* on pp. 121–122 in the COMMUNIPAK. PAIRED/GROUP ACTIVITY
Homework		Remind students that they will be taking the Unit 7 test in two days. They should begin to prepare for it.

© D.C. Heath and Company, a Division of Houghton Mifflin Company

Leçon 28: *Alice a un job*

DAY 19

TEACHING RESOURCES	TIME	STRATEGIES
Warm-up **COMMUNIPAK**	45 min.	If they have not already completed these COMMUNIPAK activities, students should work with a partner to complete the *Tu as la parole, Conversations, Échanges,* and *Tête à Tête* sections in the COMMUNIPAK, pp. 123–137. Because there are so many different activities here, you may want to change the pairs after each section. You may ask pairs to present their work to the class, or you may want to check on each pair several times throughout the period to answer questions or check on their work. **PAIRED/GROUP ACTIVITY**
Homework		Remind students to prepare for the Unit 7 test.

Leçon 28: *Alice a un job*

DAY 20

TEACHING RESOURCES	TIME	STRATEGIES

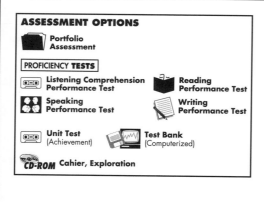

ASSESSMENT OPTIONS
- Portfolio Assessment
- **PROFICIENCY TESTS**
  - Listening Comprehension Performance Test
  - Reading Performance Test
  - Speaking Performance Test
  - Writing Performance Test
  - Unit Test (Achievement)
  - Test Bank (Computerized)
- **CD-ROM** Cahier, Exploration

At this point you may choose which testing option you want to use, depending on your teaching style and the needs and make-up of your particular class. For a Unit Test, see the Testing and Assessment Kit. There are many options available in DISCOVERING FRENCH and there is a great deal of flexibility. Depending on your teaching style and the make-up of your classroom, you may wish to use any or all of the tests shown on the left.

Administer Unit Test 7 from the Testing and Assessment Kit. This will probably take some students the entire period. While they are doing the writing part of the test, you may want to call individual students to your desk to administer the Speaking Proficiency Test.

© D.C. Heath and Company, a Division of Houghton Mifflin Company

TEACHING RESOURCES   TIME   STRATEGIES

Other Long-Term Projects

Students generate a list of Internet addresses in the Virtual Shopping Trip on p. 89 of INTERNET CONNECTION NOTES.

Additional Activity   COMMUNIPAK

Au grand magasin! Have students pair up to guess how much different clothing items cost on pp. 133–134 of the COMMUNIPAK. **PAIRED/GROUP ACTIVITY**

© D.C. Heath and Company, a Division of Houghton Mifflin Company

Your Lesson Plan

Unité/Leçon_____

Day	**Time**	**Strategies**

© D.C. Heath and Company, a Division of Houghton Mifflin Company